Managing Behaviour in the Primary School

Second Edition

Jim Docking

David Fulton Publishers
London

Published in association with the Roehampton Institute London

David Fulton Publishers Ltd
Ormond House, 26–27 Boswell Street, London WC1N 3JZ
www.fultonpublishers.co.uk

First published in Great Britain by David Fulton Publishers 1990
Second edition published in Great Britain by David Fulton
Publishers1996
Reprinted 1998, 1999, 2001

Note: The right of Jim Docking to be identified as the author of this
work has been asserted by him in accordance with the Copyright,
Designs and Patents Act 1988.

Copyright © Jim Docking

British Library Cataloguing in Publication Data
A catalogue record for this book is available from the British Library

ISBN 1–85346–397–3

Typeset by FSH Print & Production Ltd, London
Printed in Great Britain by The Cromwell Press Ltd, Trowbridge

Contents

Preface to the second edition

The second edition of this book is a general revision and up-dating of the original publication, with three new chapters on school policies. It also includes more examples of 'good practice' that I have been privileged to observe in schools. Throughout the book, new material has been introduced, but especially on ways of enhancing self-esteem, organising cooperative learning, responding to individual behaviour problems, developing a whole-school behaviour policy, managing behaviour during playtime and lunchtime, combating bullying, and engaging pupils in behaviour policy. I hope the reader will like the bigger format and the greater use of checklists and diagrams.

Jim Docking
Roehampton, December 1995

Acknowledgements

I am again most grateful for the invaluable help received from primary school heads and teachers, who have given generously of their time to talk about their approaches to managing pupil behaviour and have kindly allowed me to make observations in their schools. My special thanks are are due to the following: Richard Brading, Norma Bramley, Brenda Casey, Chris Earley, Margaret Etherington, Sr Jo Goggins, Jacquie Goodall, Krystyn Hollaway, and Timothy Rome. I wish also to thank Robin Barr, Headmaster of Hoe Bridge School, Woking, Surrey, for permission to reproduce the leaflet on bullying (pp.140–41), designed by Matthew Board, one of his pupils; Jacquie and David Coulby and Falmer Press for permission to reproduce the 'Page from a Success Book' (p.59), originally published in a book I edited called *Education and Alienation in the Junior School* (1990); and Ted Truscoe, Head Teacher of Woodville School, Leatherhead, Surrey, and Jo Rew, formerly a teacher at the school and now Deputy Head of Brockham School, Surrey, for permission to describe in detail their approach to developing a school code of behaviour (Chapter 6).

Lastly, I must thank my wife, Anne, an unfailing source of inspiration, and without whose encouragement this work would have been impossible.

The Problem of Problem Behaviour

Few matters affect teachers more directly and persistently than managing classroom behaviour. This was certainly the conclusion reached in the national survey commissioned by the Elton Committee, which was set up by the Government in March 1988 'in view of public concern about violence and indiscipline in schools and the problems faced by the teaching profession today'. Amongst the findings relating to primary school teachers, 97 per cent said that during the previous week they had had to deal with pupils talking out of turn, while 90 per cent reported pupils hindering each other and 85 per cent reported pupils making unnecessary non-verbal noise. Additionally, 60 per cent or more had had to deal with pupils wandering around the room without permission, 'calculated idleness', and general rowdiness (Gray and Simes, 1989).

Unlike the media portrayals at that time, the picture that emerged from this investigation was not one of daily physical aggression towards staff (mentioned by only 2.1 per cent) or constant verbal abuse (mentioned by only 7 per cent), though certainly some teachers had experienced violent incidents. Rather the problem was the cumulative stress-inducing effects of frequent, low-level disruption. In an important sense this gave grounds for optimism since the problem behaviours that teachers most often experience were of the kind which, given appropriate support, can normally be dealt with by improved classroom management and school ethos. Similar findings have since emerged from the Leverhulme Primary Project (Wragg, 1993) carried out between 1988 and 1992. When the observations of over 1,000 lesson segments in the classes of 48 qualified and 12 student teachers were analysed, 98 per cent of deviant behaviour was assessed as mild, and only 2 per cent as serious. But in just over half the observation sequences there was some minor misbehaviour such as (in order of frequency) unwanted talking, movement without permission, twanging a ruler or some other inappropriate use of materials, and defiance of the teacher. Interestingly, during observations of 100 lessons taken by experienced teachers, there was little difference in categories and frequencies of misbehaviour in the North-West of England, the South-West and the east end of London (except that pupils were more likely to argue with the teacher in London schools); but more misbehaviour occurred among younger junior pupils aged seven to nine than amongst infants or older juniors.

Reports from OFSTED inspectors are another source for assessing behaviour standards in schools. The 1994 Report of HM Chief Inspector, Chris Woodhead, suggested that behaviour had been rated favourably in three-quarters of primary schools and highly in half; unfavourable judgements affected about one school in 14.

Of course, broad statistics such as these mask differences in behaviour between schools in similar catchment areas. Confirming previous findings from HM Inspectorate and professional researchers, the Elton team was struck by the way in which schools in similar kinds of areas (mainly urban) could be experiencing very different levels in standards of behaviour. It seemed that although the magnitude of behaviour problems was generally greater in 'tough' areas, standards also varied according to different kinds of school policies and teacher strategies:

> When we visited schools we were struck by the differences in their 'feel' or atmosphere. Our conversations with teachers left us convinced that some schools have a more positive atmosphere than others. It was in these positive schools that we tended to see the work and behaviour which impressed us most. We found that we could not explain these different school atmospheres by saying that the pupils came from different home backgrounds. Almost all the schools we visited were in what many teachers would describe as difficult urban areas. We had to conclude that these differences had something to do with what went on in the schools themselves.
>
> *Elton Report* (DES, 1989, para. 4.1)

The Leverhulme Primary Project (Wragg, 1993) confirmed the view that social conditions, whilst affecting class management, were not its sole determinant. Even within the same school, one teacher's pupils could be on-task and orderly while another's could be characterised by deviance and low pupil application, whilst well-behaved classes could be found in unpromising environments and poorly behaved classes in idyllic surroundings.

Besides reporting on pupil-staff relationships, the survey for the Elton Committee also commented on personal behaviour *between* pupils. Here the picture of aggression was very different. Almost three in every four primary teachers said that they had had to deal with aggression between pupils in the classroom at least once during the previous week. As many as 86 per cent mentioned they they had witnessed at least one incident of physical aggression between pupils in the playground or corridors over the past week, and a large majority had encountered other kinds of inconsiderate pupil-to-pupil behaviour. More recently, findings from a survey of schools in Sheffield, prior to a project on combating bullying, have also suggested that pupil-to-pupil aggression is a matter of concern (see Chapter 8). Fortunately, later evidence demonstrated once again that school policy and ethos can make a difference in behavioural standards: in schools which subsequently had implemented a range of positive strategies to combat bullying over a period of four terms, there was a reduction in bullying – especially when the interventions were an integral part of a whole-school policy (Whitney *et al.*, 1994). In many schools, bullying was reduced by between 20 and 30 per cent, and on some indicators by as much as 50 to 80 per cent.

In short, it appears from the evidence – which is largely based on surveys in urban areas – that, although some schools do experience unacceptably high levels of ill-discipline, children's behaviour, whether in relation to staff or other pupils, can be measurably improved provided there is the commitment to implement a range of measures.

So what are the policies and strategies that appear to make for better behaviour in the classroom, the playground and elsewhere in schools? That is what this book is about. The first chapter looks at different styles of school discipline, noting which styles are usually more effective, and ends by suggesting a general framework whereby both individual teachers and the school community as a whole can review their work in improving children's behaviour. Chapters 2 to 5 then examine the four main facets of this framework:

- pre-empting behaviour problems
- reinforcing good behaviour
- developing good behaviour.
- responding to behaviour problems.

The last three chapters examine school-based, rather than classroom-based, policies, focusing on the characteristics of whole-school behaviour policies and pupils' behaviour towards each other, especially with respect to playground behaviour and bullying.

CHAPTER 1

Effective Behaviour Management

Government requirements for initial teacher training courses make clear that all successful students must have demonstrated, in the classroom, their ability to manage pupil behaviour. Newly qualified teachers should as a result be able to establish clear expectations of pupil behaviour and secure appropriate standards of discipline, so as to create and maintain an orderly classroom environment.

Pupil Behaviour and Discipline, DfE Circular 8/94, para. 28.

Like many other areas of work, teaching is riddled with its special jargon. Furthermore, the jargon is constantly changing. In curricular matters, for instance, we now speak of physical 'education' rather than, as formerly, physical 'training', and we use the term 'creative writing' instead of 'composition'. Children who experience difficulty with the curriculum are no longer 'backward' but have 'special educational needs', while every primary school must now have a body of 'governors' rather than 'managers', as previously. The jargon is also changing in matters to do with social behaviour. Traditionally, teachers have talked about 'controlling' or 'disciplining' *children*, but nowadays the phrase 'managing *behaviour*' seems to be gaining currency.

Although new educational terminology sometimes amounts to little more than new labels for old practices, it often represents a change in underlying assumptions, a redefinition of basic concepts, or a fresh approach. This is certainly the case with the curriculum and administration examples cited above, and it seems true also with respect to the term 'managing behaviour'. For many teachers today want to distance themselves from the restricted assumptions, aims and practices which are often implied in traditional talk about 'controlling' or 'disciplining' children. Of course, control is still regarded as playing an important part in regulating social behaviour because children, both for their psychological stability and their group needs, depend upon some measure of direction and a predictable social environment. By itself, however, 'control' is too restrictive a concept to do justice to the range of characteristics that contribute to effective behaviour management, while its mechanistic connotations imply that teachers order their charges without respecting their personhood. There is little room for discourse, for listening to and trying to understand the voices of the pupils. The word 'discipline' in one sense is importantly associated with 'disciple', suggesting that teachers and pupils should be working together towards an idealised kind of behaviour. However, although the term 'disciplined behaviour' has this connotation, 'disciplining children' is more often associated with 'disciplinarian' and notions of inflexible, even harsh, external control.

Figure 1.1 indicates five sets of contrasting ideas that characterise the distinction between effective behaviour management (in bold) and controlling or disciplining children (in parentheses). In examining each of these, we shall see how the shift to the expression 'managing pupil behaviour' reflects a growing desire amongst teachers to re-examine traditional policies and practices and to develop more positive approaches that are in keeping with recent concepts of good management practice.

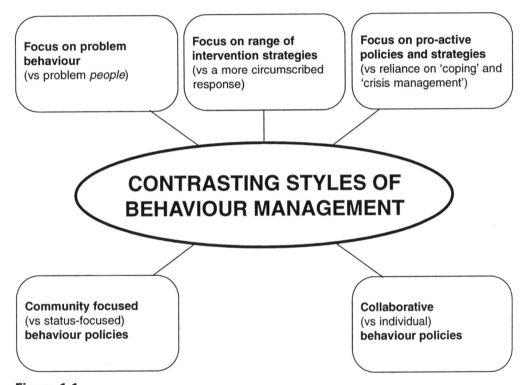

Figure 1.1

FOCUS ON PROBLEM BEHAVIOUR vs FOCUS ON PROBLEM PEOPLE

The attributional language of staffroom discussions often reveals a good deal about the assumptions teachers hold concerning the cause and nature of pupil behaviour that threatens classroom order. While some teachers personalise the situation by readily talking of 'problem pupils' or pupils who are 'naughty', 'disruptive', 'disturbed', 'devious', 'troublemakers', 'disaffected', and so on, others prefer to talk in terms of individuals' problem *behaviour* and its effects.

The term 'managing pupil behaviour' is intended convey this difference of emphasis by avoiding the suggestion that a child presenting behaviour problems is inherently a problem *person*. The trouble with using terms which imply the notion of problem people is that we may encourage those to whom we talk to slip into the habit of labelling children negatively, so that everyone no longer sees 'the child with problems' so much as the inherently 'problem pupil', 'the disruptive pupil' or 'the troublemaker'. For the language we use in describing a situation affects the way we come to conceptualise that situation, and this in turn affects our *response* to the situation. Too easily, 'problem people' becomes 'those whose behaviour we believe cannot be changed'.

Terms like 'troublemaker' and 'naughty pupil' tend to characterise problem behaviour as intentionally and malevolently produced. Such terms convey the assumption that children who are thus referred to need only to change their attitude in order to change their behaviour, and that responsibility for this rests with the child. The term 'disruptive (rather than disrupting) pupil' conveys similar assumptions. No doubt, the use of these expressions serve as a defence mechanism. For by attributing behaviour problems to the child's bad motives, teachers preserve their own status by exempting themselves from blame whilst also conveying the message that any change in their response to the behaviour is conditional upon the child taking the first step.

This was demonstrated in a study of four- to eleven-year-olds who presented problems of one kind or another in the classroom. Rohrkemper and Brophy (1983) analysed teachers' reactions to various types of learning and behaviour problems, including aggression, defiance, shyness, rejection by peers, hyperactivity, short attention span, and social immaturity. The findings showed an interesting trend: the more that the child's problem posed a threat to the classroom teacher's control, the more the teacher took the view that the child was intentionally creating the problem and that it was up to the child to control it. Teachers were prepared to develop special programmes and put themselves out for children who were rejected by their peers, who were less able (as distinct from underachieving) and who were shy or socially immature; but they tended to blame, reprimand and punish those who were aggressive, disobedient or underachieving.

Of course, if we are to regard children as persons, then we must also attribute to them intentionality and blameworthiness. To deny these attributes would be to deny children the very characteristics that make them human and capable of 'responsible' behaviour. Some children on some occasions, even in nursery and infant classes, do seem to be deliberately 'naughty' and 'out to make trouble', just as some children on some occasions seem to go out of their way to be kind and considerate. None the less, intentionality does not exist in a vacuum. Without denying that problem behaviour is often intentional and sometimes malevolent, we still need to explain how it is that some pupils seem bent on 'making trouble' and whether there is something others can do to change the conditions which seem to encourage such behaviour. Moreover, a tendency to see pupils with behaviour problems in terms of pupils with nasty intentions leads to a style of response which does little to ameliorate the problem. The teacher's classroom management becomes characterised by perpetual nagging, criticising, scolding, admonishing and sometimes punishing. Certainly children sometimes do deserve to be reprimanded and punished, but if they experience these measures as typical responses to their unwanted behaviour they come to resent the imputation of 'being bad', and this helps to maintain the problem.

Whereas the term 'troublemaker' or 'naughty pupil' conveys the idea of bad motives, the term 'problem pupil' encapsulates a different set of preconceptions. Here it is some kind of defect or illness that is taken to be the source of the problem, rather than malevolent intentions. There is, as some teachers put it, 'something wrong with the child'. This medical model has important consequences for the teacher's responsibility. Children are said to suffer from 'disorders' and therefore to be in need of 'treatment', which only 'experts' can give; and, because the teacher does not have the necessary expertise, the child must be 'referred' to someone else with the requisite professional skills, perhaps in a special unit or special school. It is not suggested here that the notion of a disordered personality has no scientific basis, nor that referrals are often inappropriate, but simply that thinking of problem behaviour in terms of 'problem pupils' can have unproductive consequences for the management of behaviour in school generally. For although one consequence of the notion of 'problem pupils' (in stark contrast to the effects of 'troublemakers' imputations) has been the development of more humane and caring attitudes, and although children have undoubtedly often been helped by the treatment received, the result of perceiving problem behaviour in this way as a matter of course is to deny the skill of teachers and parents, encouraging them to believe that they are powerless to effect a change in the behaviour themselves, even with support. Yet experience demonstrates how teachers *can* bring about remarkable changes in children's behaviour through appropriate intervention strategies.

The tendency among some teachers to assume that it must be the parents who are responsible for the problem behaviour is another example of focusing on problem people rather than on the behaviour itself. In one study among 428 junior school staff, two out of every three heads or teachers explained the behaviour problems of their pupils in terms of deficiencies in the children's home circumstances, whilst in only 3.8 per cent of cases did teachers acknowledge that the child's conduct could be attributed, at least in part, to arrangements in school or classroom management styles (Croll and Moses, 1985). The Elton Committee found a similar reaction among teachers giving reasons for discipline problems, the majority citing family instability, conflict, poverty and parental indifference or hostility to school. Of course the behaviour of many children is a reflection of their home circumstances, but this explanation is often too simplistic. In a study of 343 top infants in London (Tizard *et al.*, 1988), less than one-third of the problems seen by teachers in school had also been seen by parents at home, while only just over one-third of the problems raised by parents had also been noted in school. As the Elton Committee noted:

> Researchers have consistently found that when parents and teachers are asked to identify children with behaviour problems in a class they identify roughly the same number, *but they are largely different children*. The overlap is small. Parents who tell the headteacher that their child 'doesn't behave like that at home' are likely to be telling the truth. Our evidence suggests that many heads and teachers tend to underestimate or even ignore the school-based factors involved in disruptive behaviour.

> (DES, 1989, para 4.145, emphasis added)

Thus while some children's behaviour in school is, at least in part, a consequence of adverse home circumstances, it is misleading to assume that they are the only explanations or even the main ones. As we can all testify from everyday experience, the way individuals behave is affected by the *context* in which the behaviour is manifest. Just as most of us feel better when the weather is warm and sunny or when we are in the company of people we like or even if we are in a certain room or building, so the behaviour of a child in school is materially affected by matters such as the teacher's expectations of the child's behaviour, the teacher's classroom management and teaching styles, curriculum opportunities and the general ethos of the school.

A danger of focusing on problem people rather than problem behaviour is that teachers and schools may fail to pay sufficient attention to the contribution they themselves are making to maintain, and even generate, the problem behaviour. To see children who present behaviour problems as 'troublemakers' is to imply that it is the child who has to accept the main responsibility for changing the problem behaviour; to see such children as 'problem pupils' is to imply that only the expert can help; and to lay the blame at the door of 'problem parents' is to assume that it is the parent who must take the initiative. Certainly there are many factors, such as those 'within' the child or in the home, which are outside the immediate control of teachers and may predispose the child to behave disruptively in school. But the extent to which a child realises such a tendency depends upon the quality of life experienced in school. For instance, children who come from homes where there is a high level of stress due to disharmony, may or may not use the school to vent frustration, depending on how they believe they are valued and have status in the school community. Moreover, the manner in which children presenting behaviour problems are treated in school affects the degree to which their adverse family circumstances affect them, a point recognised in the Department for Education Circular on pupil behaviour:

> For some pupils, the school may be the only secure, stable environment. It has been shown that, when children have relationships outside the family in which they feel valued and respected, this helps to protect them against adversity within the family.
>
> (DfE, 1994a, para. 50)

FOCUS ON A RANGE OF INTERVENTION STRATEGIES vs A MORE CIRCUMSCRIBED RESPONSE

Fortunately, more and more teachers are subscribing to a model which recognises the multifaceted nature of behaviour problems in school. They acknowledge the *range* of factors that could be affecting pupil behaviour and they therefore minimise the risk of too easily laying the blame – and therefore the responsibility for change – at one door. Children's behaviour is the product of a number of interacting factors and the relative importance of each varies from one child to another.

In the *systems model* of pupil behaviour, children in school are seen as functioning within a network of inter-related systems such as the family, the peer group, the classroom, the playground and the school at large. Each system is made up of interacting elements, or aspects of the situation, which influence, and are often influenced by, the child's behaviour. Thus in the classroom, the elements clearly include the pupils and the teacher, but they also incorporate the curriculum, the resources, the way children are grouped, the rules, furniture layout, and so on – all affecting the child's behaviour and often being affected by it. The playground can also be regarded as a system whose elements not only comprise the pupils in the child's own classroom, but also children from other classes. Other elements in the playground system are the playground supervisors, the space available, facilities for play, the design of the playground, and playground customs, rules and sanctions. In the school at large, the elements comprise all the pupils, all the staff and the head, plus the school rules and expectations, the procedures for assembly, the length of lessons and playtimes, the layout of the buildings, specialist facilities, and so on, where again influences work in all directions. The family, neighbourhood and peer group systems contain further sets of elements operating in this interactive way.

The systems model thus encourages us to view the child's behaviour as a function of numerous interacting elements in various overlapping systems. The practical implications of this are important. To bring about any significant change among pupils presenting problem behaviour, it is clearly not enough to use one strategy; rather the approach must involve changing the nature of the key elements that make up the various systems in which the child operates. Intervention is therefore taken at a *number of levels* to take account of the range of elements that affect the child's behaviour in school. In contrast to models of behaviour that are seen in terms of problem people (as examined in the previous section) adherence to the systems model does not entail the belief that all the responsibility for change in pupils' behaviour must lie with just one party, whether it is the pupils, parents, teachers, support services, or 'society'. All parties are responsible. However, since the problem behaviour occurs in the school, the *initiative* needs to be taken by teachers. Naturally, it is those elements within the school system and its sub-systems (classrooms, corridors, playground, lunchroom) which will receive the most attention, but collaboration with parents and maybe other members of the community will have a vital part to play. The systems model also importantly recognises that behaviour problems can often be the outward manifestations of other undiagnosed difficulties such as learning, receptive language, borderline communication or even sensory impairment (Gasgoigne, 1994). Intervention strategies will therefore very likely need to include measures which address such underlying issues.

FOCUS ON PRO-ACTIVE POLICIES AND STRATEGIES vs RELIANCE ON 'COPING' AND 'CRISIS MANAGEMENT'

A crucial aspect of effective behaviour management is a determination to stand back and examine pedagogic and classroom management styles. The inclusion of 'pedagogic' as well as 'management' styles here is important since the two are inter-related. As we saw at the end of the last section, there is a strong overlap between factors that contribute to effective pupil learning and factors that contribute to acceptable pupil behaviour. Official guidance from the Department for Education seems somewhat confused about this, but implicitly recognises the chicken-and-egg situation: 'It stands to reason that, if teachers do not keep order, the children in their charge will not learn well'; yet three sentences before it was acknowledged that 'where classroom teaching is good, discipline problems in class are fewer'! (DfE, 1994a, para 28).

Traditional notions of 'control' or 'discipline' have tended to involve the idea that teachers who are successful in achieving orderly behaviour are those whose management styles consist essentially of measures to keep a tight rein on classes by reprimanding and punishing children as they step out of line. In recent years, this notion has been challenged by evidence from classroom observation studies. Much of the research originates in the United States, but the ideas are gaining currency in this country. They were clearly recognised in the Elton Report (DES, 1989), and have again been emphasised in more recent official guidance (DfE, 1994a).

A particularly important finding is that successful classroom managers are those who adopt pro-active strategies by *pre-empting behaviour problems*. The seminal work on this issue was undertaken by Jacob Kounin of Wayne State University. The problem he investigated concerned a fact which we all know: that pupils behave better with some teachers than with others. By analysing videotapes of many lessons in elementary schools, Kounin (1970) soon found that the most effective teachers were not necessarily those who were most ready to reprimand and punish culprits, and certainly not those who relied on 'crisis management' strategies to deal with misbehaviour once it had occurred: rather they were those who anticipated behaviour problems by taking measures to prevent them arising in the first place. Following from this work, various researchers in the USA and the UK have confirmed Kounin's findings, and have identified a number of key group management skills which make all the difference to the quality of classroom behaviour. We shall examine these in the next chapter.

Another major challenge to the idea that orderly class behaviour is essentially a function of efficient negative reactive strategies comes from behavioural psychology. According to the Law of Effect, an action is more likely to be repeated if the perpetrator finds it a rewarding experience. In the classroom, attention-seeking behaviour will often unwittingly be reinforced because such behaviour has pay-off for the pupils concerned – that is, they get the recognition they are seeking from the teacher and the other children, even if this takes the form of negative attention. The culprit is thus given status: being bad is being somebody. Wise teachers, however, seize on the *wanted* behaviour of children and ensure that this is *reinforced* through praise or reward. As the Elton Committee noted, bad behaviour is then marginalised. The system of strategies which has been developed to implement this policy is encapsulated in the phrase 'catch the child being good'. The features of this positive approach to classroom behaviour are discussed in Chapter 3. Of course, teachers still need strategies to deal with incidents of undesirable behaviour, but the manner of their reprimanding and their punishment styles will be more constructive; non-punitive intervention strategies such as special programmes of work or counselling are used in appropriate cases. In a sense, therefore, their approach to correcting children's behaviour is also positive. This is the subject of Chapter 5.

Parallel with the policy of reinforcing good behaviour is that of *developing* good behaviour in the first place. In recent years, a wealth of research has demonstrated the impact of teachers' verbal and non-verbal language on children's evaluations of themselves – their sense of self-worth, their motivation to learn and their beliefs about their capabilities. By what they say and don't say, and by what they do and don't do, teachers set up positive or negative expectations for achievement. They enhance or deflate pupils' self-esteem, and they influence pupils' feelings of competence and confidence. These aspects of the 'hidden' curriculum have direct relevance to children's learning opportunities, but they are also linked to their classroom behaviour. Children who sense that their teacher holds positive expectations about their learning potential and values them as persons are going to feel better about themselves. They will therefore feel less need to indulge in acting out behaviour to gain status and to compensate for beliefs in their inadequacy. Instead they will be more inclined to cooperate to demonstrate that the teacher's positive expectations are justified. As we shall see in Chapter 4, there are also specific strategies which teachers can employ to help children to think more positively about themselves and to encourage self-discipline and a spirit of cooperation.

COMMUNITY-FOCUSED vs STATUS-FOCUSED POLICIES

Effective behaviour management is as much about the quality of *relationships between pupils* as with pupils' conduct in relation to authority figures. It includes a concern for children's individual predicaments and welfare needs as well as the needs of the school as an institution. The current concern with bullying in schools is an example of a problem which has not been adequately addressed in traditional 'control' approaches which focus unduly on the institutional needs of the school. A school's behaviour policy must address issues which include aggressive playground behaviour, hurtful teasing and ostracising others. In the classroom teachers must try to deepen children's understanding of their own behaviour and its effect on others and also employ strategies to encourage greater cooperation between pupils. These aspects of behaviour management are discussed in Chapters 7 and 8.

COLLABORATIVE vs INDIVIDUAL BEHAVIOUR POLICIES

Although head teachers and governors have the statutory overall responsibility for the school's behaviour policy, and although individual teachers have the responsibility to keep order, the concept of effective behaviour management assumes that decision-making should be *shared*.

We saw earlier that the systems model of pupil behaviour involves the notion of *interacting* elements. This being so, it follows that changing any one element in the school system could have implications for other elements. For example, a change to staggered playtimes to alleviate playground problems has implications for the length of lessons, which in turn has implications for curriculum opportunities, which again could have implications for pupil behaviour. Hence it is essential that there are whole-school policies which take account of the uniqueness of the school's situation and the inter-relatedness of elements which make up that situation.

Without the support of colleagues, it is sometimes easier for teachers to stick doggedly to familiar control practices even when they are manifestly not working. For instance, some teachers continue to nag and shout at individuals or the class even though these actions are winding the pupils up and provoking more of the behaviour which the teachers are trying to stamp out. By contrast, successful class managers are more prepared to engage in self-appraisal, to experiment with new approaches and to change practices in the light of experience. They are, if you like, researchers in their own classrooms. However, this reappraisal is best undertaken collaboratively with colleagues rather than alone. Classroom control has traditionally been left to the initiative of individual teachers, perhaps with the option of sending pupils to the head or another senior member of staff. The understanding has been that to seek the support of colleagues, other than by 'referring upwards' or having a moan in the staffroom, would be to signal professional incompetence. As David Hargreaves (1978, p.541) once put it, 'Teachers bear their stress in painful isolation'. Consequently some teachers would rather be ineffective than develop skills through constructive discussion with colleagues. The trend today, however, is towards a spirit of communal support among staff. Teachers who are interested in improving their classroom relationships know that they have much to learn from each other and that they will receive much moral support if problems are shared. Indeed, the Elton Report recommended the formation of staff support groups to achieve just this end.

The writer once asked a primary head if she had a whole-school policy for behaviour. 'Oh yes, indeed,' came the reply, 'I wrote it during the summer holidays.' The policy document was certainly comprehensive and positive, and it had been submitted to all staff for their consideration. None the less, for all the amendments and fine tuning, it was regarded by everyone else as essentially the head's instructions. A genuine whole-school policy is not only *about* the whole school but is *drawn up* by the whole school. This involves the active participation not only of all the adults who work in the school, including support and non-teaching staff such as playground supervisors, but also governors, parents, and – most importantly – the pupils themselves. Management in this context certainly includes leadership from the head, but it is the kind of leadership which arrests apathy, sets up mechanisms for discussion, delegates coordinating responsibilities, facilitates the communication and exchange of ideas between different parts of the school community, and engenders an attitude of mind which encourages everybody to consider ideas no matter how much they challenge time-honoured approaches.

Although the research team appointed by the Elton Committee asked teachers to explain behaviour problems which they faced in school, they did not conduct any investigation to find out what pupils thought, even at secondary level. This is surprising in view of the Committee's recommendations that 'head teachers and teachers should give pupils every opportunity to take responsibilities and to make a full contribution to improving behaviour in school' (para. 6.8). The central role of pupils in developing behaviour policy is recognised in the DfE Circular on school discipline:

> Many schools have found that pupils can play a positive role; for example in exposing bullying in their school, in helping to design play areas, and in suggesting strategies to deal with problematic situations (e.g. arrangements for pupils in wet playtimes). Schools' councils and other participative approaches are possible means of encouraging pupils to become involved.
>
> (DfE, 1994a, para 22)

Some people argue that primary school pupils are too young to have coherent and rational views about the management of their individual and group behaviour, and that it would therefore be improper to let them have a say. This position is understandable. Even in the upper junior classes, children often lack the social maturity to see problems from various points of view and to predict the consequences of their decisions. There is another consideration too: pupil participation involves a willingness to redistribute the power bases in the school – and that can be threatening for some teachers.

However, there are three main reasons for believing that the gradual involvement of pupils is appropriate in decisions relating to their behaviour. The first is that it works. Nowhere has this been clearer than in the DfE-sponsored project to develop strategies to combat bullying and improve playground behaviour (Sharp and Smith, 1994; Smith and Sharp, 1994), aspects of which we shall examine in the last two chapters. For provided children are given a clear framework in which to participate, they take behaviour issues seriously and make constructive contributions to such matters as classroom rules, a playground code and measures to counter bullying.

The second reason is a managerial one. As the Elton Report recognised, it is through eliciting their active involvement as initiators of ideas that children feel committed to policies and to the school community.

Thirdly, engaging children in debate about school behaviour is valuable in its own right as part of their social and moral education. Effective behaviour management involves teachers being sensitive to children's perceptions of behaviour problems and to such matters as classroom and playground rules. They want to develop pupils' *understanding* of policies which regulate individual freedom, protect minority interests, and promote the common good.

These notions do not just develop naturally in children, but arise through their interactions with peers and adults and through experiencing the consequences of decision-making. Involving pupils also contributes to children's emotional development, helping them to refine their feelings about their own and others' behaviour. Staff must always look to their motives for involving children, and any decision to involve them must never be just tokenism but an educational opportunity.

The role of teachers in eliciting the involvement of the children in behaviour matters, far from being peripheral, is central to effective behaviour management. There are, of course, dangers. One is allowing children to participate, but then not following up their suggestions or simply dismissing them as impractical. Another is failing to match the degree of involvement to the children's achievement level. If this is pitched too low or too high, the children will become frustrated and disappointed. Arnstein (1969) has produced a 'ladder' of participation in which the bottom rungs amount to tokenism and the top ones to increasing degrees of true participation. Thus pupils may be informed, consulted, or invited to join a school committee, but genuine empowerment involves more than this. It entails the concepts of *partnership* (whereby pupils are invited to accept equal responsibility for decisions), *delegation* (whereby pupils are given specific powers to make decisions) and *control* (total responsibility). On this argument, school staffs need to ask themselves at what level they feel it appropriate to pitch pupil involvement in the development of behaviour policy. It is unlikely they will invite pupils to assume total control (though there could be some carefully defined areas of policy-making where this might be possible, at least for older juniors), but unless the involvement is at the 'partnership' or 'delegation' levels, pupil involvement does not amount to a genuine participatory approach. Chapters 6, 7 and 8 explore some possibilities.

What about the involvement of parents? In traditional school regimes, parents are frequently involved to the extent that they are told about such matters as school rules, uniform, and the system of punishments and rewards. However, even at the level of being informed, teachers have not always involved parents in matters related to the behaviour of their children. Effective behaviour management entails a recognition of the *right* of parents to receive information and be given opportunities to discuss both school behaviour policy in general and the actions of their child in particular. Parents need to have easy access to the head and they need to know that their perspective will be welcomed and treated as valid. Some schools also regard home-visiting as an integral, if time-consuming, component of effective home-school liaison.

More and more primary schools are now *working with* parents in a spirit of partnership. Parent involvement in reading and other areas of the curriculum is now widespread and its benefits are well recognised, not only in terms of the children's intellectual development but also in terms of their attitude to school and motivation to learn (Docking, 1990). Parents may also be involved in behaviour matters more directly, participating with teachers in working out behaviour policy (for example, over approaches to bullying and playground behaviour) and cooperating in the monitoring of the child's behaviour in school.

'BEING POSITIVE'

In this chapter we have seen that there are a variety of ways in which heads and their staffs can 'be positive', as the jargon goes nowadays. This phrase is sometimes associated specifically with reinforcing children's behaviour through praise and rewards; but it is clear from our discussion that 'being positive' encompasses a great range of policies and strategies.

This is shown in Checklist 1.1, which suggests a possible framework for developing positive behaviour policies. Boxes 1 and 2 are concerned with unwanted behaviour, Boxes 3 and 4 with wanted behaviour. Boxes 1 and 3 relate to strategies which come into play *before* the behaviour (either wanted or unwanted) is manifest, Boxes 2 and 4 relate to strategies which *respond* to behaviour (either problem behaviour or good behaviour). Between them, the boxes in this two-way grid thus generate four key questions, as shown, all of which need addressing for effective behaviour management. The checklists suggest examples of the particular matters over which policies and strategies need to be developed by individual teachers or the school as a whole. It must be noted, however, that the allocation of an item to one box rather than another does not mean that it has no relevance to the questions in the other boxes: there is a good deal of overlap. For instance, punishment issues are placed in Box 2 (response to unwanted behaviour); but, since punishing may be a deterrent as well as retributive action, it might also have been included in Box 1. Similarly, praise matters are placed in Box 4 (reinforcement of good behaviour), but could also have been inserted in Box 1 since praising children often has what Kounin (1970) called a 'ripple effect' on other children's behaviour, and so helps to pre-empt behaviour problems.

That positive strategies can and do make a difference is undeniable. In his report on the Leverhulme Primary Project, Wragg (1993) compares the dissimilar behaviour of two junior classes in the *same* school with children of similar social background. The low levels of task involvement and above-average incidence of misbehaviour in Miss Baker's class is attributed to the absence of a positive approach, particularly with respect to two factors:

● the rules of behaviour were not clear or consistently applied, with harsh enforcement one moment and ignoring misbehaviour the next

- generally negative relationships compared with the successful teacher, with little recognition of good work or behaviour.

The first point is illustrated by examples such as giving instructions but not ensuring they are carried out, issuing a threat ('I'm not going to tell you again, young man'), but then ignoring the next incident, asking children to put their hands up before answering but not ensuring this procedure is followed, asking a child to go out into the corridor but then ignoring him when he does not move. The second point is illustrated by examples such as being critical of two target boys, even when they are not misbehaving, shouting at children, changing her mind about instructions, and praise used only rarely.

In contrast, Mrs Abel's success in achieving high work involvement and good behaviour is explained according to these factors:

- a lot of thought about appropriate work for the class and for individuals
- copious use of reinforcement, with much use of praise, both private and public
- classroom rules consistently applied and enforced 'in a benign but firm manner'
- displaying good humour, even in trying circumstances, 'which defuses potential trouble and cements positive relationships'
- reminding pupils of the time available and regular monitoring of their work.

Among the examples used to illustrate these points are: consistently applying a rule that children waiting for help should read a book, not sit doing nothing; public recognition of achievement through inviting the class to applaud individuals who had made special progress and extensively displaying children's work; reassuring a child not certain about the answer to a question by saying patiently 'Don't panic'; and diffusing a potential confrontation by remarking humorously, 'Jason, it won't help if you're chopping her neck off with a ruler'.

In the next four chapters we shall be discussing the kinds of classroom management strategies that enabled Mrs Abel to succeed where Miss Baker manifestly did not, using the framework suggested in the checklist. The last three chapters extend the argument by applying similar principles to whole-school policies, the playground and pupils relationships with each other.

Checklist 1.1 A Framework for Developing School and Classroom Behaviour Policy

	BEFORE behaviour occurs	**AFTER behaviour occurs**
UNWANTED behaviour	① **What strategies could pre-empt unwanted behaviour?** ✔ agreed codes of behaviour for school, classroom and playground ✔ measures to generate an ethos of purposefulness ✔ effective body language and use of voice ✔ attention to classroom layout and appearance ✔ pupil grouping ✔ positive beginnings to lessons ✔ clear structures for supporting individuals ✔ effective management of critical points in lessons ✔ regular feedback to whole class ✔ attention to the school's physical environment ✔ attention to playground/lunchroom arrangements ✔ preventative strategies to combat bullying ✔ working closely with parents	② **What are the most effective ways of responding to unwanted behaviour?** ✔ attention to reprimanding style ✔ effective management of incipient confrontations ✔ provision for counselling individuals ✔ special intervention programmes for individuals ✔ an understanding of the management of hyperactivity ✔ agreed procedures for referals to senior staff and outside agencies ✔ attention to types of punishments given ✔ attention to ways of supporting and protecting victims of bullying ✔ attention to styles of response to bullying incidents ✔ agreed procedures for involving parents ✔ training of playground supervisors in dealing with unwanted behaviour
WANTED behaviour	③ **How can good behaviour be developed?** ✔ staff role models to encourage mutual respect ✔ staff communicating positive expectations of behaviour ✔ measures to enhance self-esteem, confidence and competence ✔ weekly circle times ✔ teaching children communication skills for dealing with personal incidents non-aggressively ✔ plenty for children to do at playtime ✔ experiences in cooperative learning ✔ structures whereby pupils can participate in developing behaviour policy – e.g. through Quality Circles or a school council	④ **How can good behaviour be reinforced?** ✔ a school and classroom ethos which places more emphasis on encouraging good behaviour than on reprimand and punishment ✔ effective use of praise ✔ agreed policies for rewarding children ✔ agreed structures whereby playground supervisors can reinforce good behaviour ✔ communicating with parents about special efforts

CHAPTER 2

Pre-empting Behaviour Problems

> We conclude that the central problem of disruption could be significantly reduced by helping teachers to become more efficient classroom managers.
>
> *Elton Report*, p.12

Consider the following statement given by a teacher during a creative writing lesson:

> Listen everyone [voice projected and hand raised]. Just stop what you're doing. [Pause while quickly scanning the class; then voice drops in volume.] Everyone look this way. I want you to hear what Dawn and Garry have written. They've got some interesting ideas which I think we should discuss.

In the first three sentences, the teacher, both in what she says and what she does, is using a management strategy to attract everyone's attention. The last two sentences say something about the kind of relationships she wants to develop, while the whole statement is an aspect of her teaching style which puts a premium on classroom discussion. This short extract illustrates the interdependence of effective teaching, respectful relationships and classroom management skills, as illustrated in the following diagram:

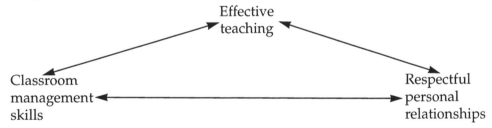

In discussing pre-emptive behavioural management skills, it is important to remember the relation between these three aspects of classroom performance. For classroom management is not something that temporally precedes effective teaching and personal relationships: the three are inseparably linked. To discuss the management of classroom behaviour will inevitably involve comments on teaching skills and inter-personal relationships.

From the evidence cited in the previous chapter, and using the framework suggested in Checklist 1.1 (Box 1), it seems that teachers who are successful in managing children's behaviour are those who, among other things, anticipate the kinds of circumstances when problem behaviour could arise and accordingly take pre-emptive measures. This chapter reviews some of the main preventative strategies which should be part of every teacher's classroom management repertoire. These can be grouped under the following headings.

- classroom rules
- planning lessons to generate purposefulness
- positive beginnings to lessons
- communicating confidence and enthusiasm through body language and use of voice
- engendering work involvement
- classroom layout and pupil grouping

CLASSROOM RULES

Rules are integral to the well-being of any institution. In his study of pupils' perception of rules, Cullingford (1988) showed clearly that by the time children reach the end of their primary education they take the need for rules for granted. Of course, children may feel that teachers sometimes unfairly apply rules of behaviour, but they do not question the *principle* that schools must have rules. As one top junior boy put it, 'If we didn't have school rules, this place would be upside down'. The Leverhulme Study on primary teaching skills (Wragg, 1993) also showed how even the younger pupils are able to relate to their teachers' rules. Not surprisingly, however, the same study revealed how student teachers often demonstrate less clarity about classroom rules and the limits of unacceptable behaviour than their experienced colleagues: when a class had no clear rules, relationships were poor and children would 'test the limits' to see what they could get away with.

Apart from those which govern general behaviour in the school, rules for individual classrooms constitute one way of pre-empting misbehaviour. They help to establish a framework in which children are helped to understand what counts as acceptable and unacceptable conduct. Classroom rules also give a set of criteria for acceptable behaviour to which teachers can easily refer in reminding children of what is expected of them.

In developing rules for the classroom, the teacher needs to address a number of issues: What should the rules be about? How many rules should there be? How should they be formulated? Should they be imposed, or should the children have a say? How should they be communicated and enforced? As regards these first questions, classroom rules need to serve three overlapping needs:

1 To ensure safety and personal welfare.
2 To provide effective conditions for teaching and learning.
3 To help children develop considerate behaviour and respect for property.

Hence rules often cover the following issues:

- entering, leaving and moving around the room;
- access to and care of materials and equipment;
- talking and listening;
- treating others as you would like them to treat you;
- making the room a pleasant place to be in.

Checklist 2.1
Effective classroom rules

Rules should be:
✓ few in number (5 is plenty)
✓ negotiated with the pupils
✓ explicit
✓ positively phrased
✓ community orientated ('We will ...')
✓ realistic (perhaps 'We will try ...' for the
   younger children).

And remember to:
✓ display rules
✓ issue reminders before an activity
✓ review from time to time.

Checklist 2.1 summarises the main criteria for effective classroom rule-making. To begin with, it helps if formal rules are few in number, say four or five. This not only makes it easier for children to remember them but also focuses on the issues you feel are particularly important for that group of children at that particular time. Later on in the term, as the class learns to live up to the rules and demonstrates a readiness to develop more sophisticated social skills, new rules can be introduced and previous ones removed. A small number of rules also minimises the risk of endless reprimand: the more rules you have, the more possible their infringement.

Some teachers believe it is better to have just one or two rules which lay down general principles of behaviour and so cover many sorts of eventualities. A rule such as 'We will try to be courteous at all times' or 'We will try to respect each other' are examples. However, there are limits to how far young children will achieve orderly conduct without also the help of precise rules for everyday matters such as movement and talking. Rules which spell out in concrete terms exactly what is expected help children to develop an understanding of what abstract phrases such as 'being courteous' or 'having respect' amounts to in practice. It is through giving children – particularly the younger ones – specific guidance that you can encourage the development of good habits. A suitable compromise, especially for older juniors, is to give the specific rules an overall title which states the general principle governing the rules. For example, a title such as 'Being considerate' would be useful as a title for rules such as 'We will try to work quietly so as not to disturb others'.

Pupils like to know where they are, and it is therefore important, on first meeting a class, for the teacher to make explicit the kind of behaviour that is expected. Additionally, taking care over the way rules are worded will help pupils to observe them more willingly and regularly. A lengthy list of 'must nots' encourages defiance and does nothing to promote an understanding of what counts as 'good behaviour'. Constructive relationships with the children are therefore more likely to be promoted if the rules are generally phrased in terms of the behaviour wanted rather than the behaviour not wanted.

It also helps if each rule is prefaced by 'We will' to signify a communal commitment rather than an imposed imperative. For example, 'We will listen carefully when the teacher is speaking' would be preferable to 'Listen carefully to the teacher' and certainly better than 'No talking when the teacher is speaking'. There are some rules where total compliance for young children might be an unreasonable expectation, for example a rule about always working quietly. In such cases, it helps if the initial words of the rule consist of 'We will try' (e.g. 'We will try to be quiet when working on our own'). This formulation sets more realistic objectives and appears more manageable.

The nature of classroom rules and the procedure for establishing them will vary from one age group to another. In the following account, a teacher in an inner-city infant school explains what she does with her Reception class:

> Most children at this age won't have experienced a large group, so we need rules to help them work happily without squabbling. For example, in my class we have a rule to regulate the number of children who can engage in any one activity. We say, 'Only two should be in the home corner, only two with the sand or water, only three with the lego or train, and so on'. This is important because it *pre-empts hassle*. Then we have a rule about being tidy: 'We will put things away where we found them'.
>
> A third rule concerns noise levels: 'We will try to be very quiet in the book corner'. We don't have a general 'no talking' rule because for some things, like the home corner, talk is needed. Making silence specific to the book corner helps children to learn when talking would hinder them and when it is appropriate. I also make it clear that there is one occasion when I must not be interrupted, and that is when I share reading with a child.
>
> Also, when I introduce rules and issue reminders, I'm careful to discuss the rationale so that children understand why the rule is needed.

As children move through the junior years, teachers can increasingly engage them in discussion about the kinds of rules which are needed to meet the needs of the class. Indeed, in some schools the agreed rules are not only displayed on the classroom walls but signed by every child in the class as an acknowledgement and public reminder that the rules have been agreed. Practice in rule-making contributes to children's social education. The process of discussion, explaining, justifying and revising suggestions helps to generate understanding and a positive attitude towards rules. However, children need help in generating their classroom rules. Left to their own devices, younger children especially will tend to suggest negative and imperative statements, with plenty of 'must nots' and 'don'ts'. The teacher needs to provide a clear framework which helps the class to identify issues, prioritise them and formulate them in terms of behaviour wanted rather than not wanted.

With her class of seven- to eight-year-olds, one teacher was observed proceeding on the following lines at the beginning of the autumn term. She began by writing on the board 'What would make our class a happy and nice place to be in?', and asking for suggestions. After a free exchange of ideas, the teacher focused on certain issues which had emerged in the discussion and wrote these on the board using the children's own formulations: 'Not talking when working', 'Not running', 'Listening carefully', 'Keeping the room tidy'. She then asked the class to suggest how the first two could be worded 'so that we all know what to do, not just what not to do'. Following the children's suggestions, these rules were changed to 'Working quietly' and 'Moving quietly'. The teacher then set the class some writing centred on the stimulus question which she had written on the board at the start and some children later read out what they had written. She later used the children's ideas to make a poster, which read:

Keeping our class a happy place

- We will try to work quietly so as not to disturb others.
- We will listen carefully when the teacher is talking to us.
- We will move quietly round the room, and walk.
- We will put litter in the bin.

This teacher also appreciated that opportunities should be taken to revise rules as needs and circumstances change. This helps children to learn to regard a set of rules as a flexible instrument which can be altered by agreement to meet personal and institutional needs more effectively. In this way, the children's involvement in rule-making is not a one-off activity, but one which is constantly maintained as the utility of the rules is monitored. So at about half-term the teacher again engaged the children in discussion about their rules, asking if any should be changed or added. On this occasion, the class decided that the second rule should have a phrase added so that the new formulation was as follows: 'We will listen carefully when the teacher is talking to us and we will listen to each other in discussion'. This reflected the fact that the teacher had been organising activities which involved collaborative learning when 'listening to each other' was very important. The children also decided that the last rule was now unnecessary since everybody now used the litter bin as a matter of course and reminders had not been needed. At the same time, resource areas in the room were getting rather messy. So the class decided to replace the fourth rule with a more general one, though still about tidiness: 'We will try to keep everywhere neat and tidy'.

By the time children are in the upper junior classes, they are able to take more initiative themselves. This is how one teacher explained how she organised rule-making with her 10– to 11–year-olds in a series of stages:

1. The children were put in groups of six and given ten minutes to devise a set of classroom rules which we all had to follow.
2. We then collated the ideas, which I listed on the board. At this stage, no one was allowed to comment.
3. Then, back in their groups, the children were asked to prioritise the rules. We found ten that were common to most groups.
4. The whole class then voted for the five rules they thought were most important. In the event, these centred round the concept of 'respect', so we decided on one general rule – 'We will show respect for each other' – to introduce the specific rules.
5. With a group of five children during an activity period, we talked about the way the rules could be worded, and two of the children then made a poster which we put on the wall. This was headed by the general rule and then the specific ones:

We will show respect for each other by:

- speaking one at a time
- listening carefully to each other and the teacher
- respecting each other's possessions
- each being responsible for keeping the room tidy
- voting on ways of working in groups when we can't agree.

6. Three children made a poster to display the rules, and every child signed this, thus making a kind of contract.

An interesting point about the third rule was that this included the teacher respecting the children's possessions: for instance she always asked the child's permission before taking something from the child's tray.

Although involving children in making classroom rules is likely to give them a sense of ownership, they will need reminding about their commitments from time to time. The skill here is reminding without scolding. Of course, there will be a place for reprimanding where this is thought deserved, but constant bickering will almost certainly be resented and lead to a deterioration in classroom relationships. In a major survey of London junior schools (Mortimore *et al.*, 1988), behaviour was found to be better in classes where teachers managed to be firm without continual intervention and nagging – authoritative without being authoritarian. For not only does perpetual telling-off create general frustration and an unpleasant atmosphere, it reinforces young children's tendency to think of rules as adult impositions, the purpose of obeying them being to avoid the adult's displeasure. Successful management of pupil behaviour depends on creating a positive climate in which children do not just try to keep on good terms with the teacher but understand that observing rules helps to provide a better atmosphere for learning and makes the classroom a happier place.

How, then, can children be reminded about rules of behaviour without resorting to regular reprimanding? One way is to display the rules and discuss them periodically, drawing attention particularly just before the start of an activity to those rules which are going to be particularly important for that occasion. The phrasing of the teacher's remarks can be important here in drawing attention to the fact that the rule has been drawn up collaboratively. The author observed one teacher doing this with effect by saying 'You remember that we agreed that...', thus avoiding remarks such as 'Now I don't want to see anyone...', which unnecessarily personalises the issue and sets a negative tone for the lesson. In another room, the reception class teacher was carefully rehearsing the rule pertaining to using paints and brushes as she started an activity. Here it was interesting to see how the reminding ended on a positive note: 'Now go and *enjoy* yourselves'.

Another 'reminding' strategy is to include rules and their justification as part of normal teaching. For instance, the teacher could remind children of a listening rule as she starts to explain or instruct. She might say: 'Now, listen carefully everyone so that you all know what to do', or 'When everyone is ready we can all enjoy this story', or 'Attend carefully now because this point is a bit complicated'.

Lastly, it is important to praise children who are observing the rules, being careful to specify the conduct to which you are drawing attention. The effect is to send round the room a 'ripple effect', other children too getting the message.

PLANNING FOR PURPOSEFULNESS

As we have seen, a key characteristic of effective behaviour management is pre-empting behaviour problems which could occur through children being bored, confused or frustrated. Boredom can arise when children feel insufficiently stimulated or challenged, or are left too long on a particular task, or are given insufficient feedback about their progress. Confusion can occur if children are not clear about what is expected of them or how to proceed or what to do next.

Frustration can ensue if the task is too difficult, or if the materials, books and teacher's support are not easily accessible.

To pre-empt these conditions, good classroom managers plan their lessons to help engender an atmosphere of *purposefulness*. The children not only feel challenged and know what is expected of them but are given the means to meet the challenge and expectations. Purposefulness also presupposes that the teacher makes effective use of time. According to research by Alexander (1992), primary children on average spend about 59 per cent of time working, 11 per cent in routine activities, 8 per cent waiting for the teacher or other adult support, and 21 per cent being distracted. Two important management considerations seem to follow from these findings. One is that teachers need to establish clearly-understood routines to minimise pupils' time-wasting (e.g. for starting and finishing lessons, tidying up, getting help); the other is that teachers must plan their work to make the best use of their own time (e.g. ensuring that sufficient time is set aside for critical feedback, which can so easily get neglected).

Checklist 2.2 and the following questions and comments indicate some of the ways in which purposefulness can be achieved through effective lesson planning and so reduce the occasion for misbehaviour.

> ### Checklist 2.2
> ### Planning for Purposefulness
>
> *Plan to provide:*
> - ✓ varied and realistically demanding tasks
> - ✓ easy access to materials and resources
> - ✓ positive work-focused lesson beginnings
> - ✓ effective support strategies
> - ✓ well thought-out ways of managing critical points
> - ✓ opportunity for feedback on pupils' work

1 *Are the pupils being given plenty to do and a variety of activities?*

An important finding of the survey of 50 London junior schools (Mortimore *et al.*, 1988) was that the better-behaved classes tended to be those in which there was an unmistakable atmosphere of work. By this was not meant busyness for its own sake ('keeping them occupied'), but purposeful busyness which reflected the fact that the children felt actively involved in realistically demanding tasks. In these circumstances, pupils enjoyed their work more, were more eager to start new activities, made less noise and moved around the room less often and more sensibly.

One way of achieving such an atmosphere of work is to ensure that, over the course of a week, and to some extent the day and each session, the children are engaged in a variety of tasks so that different sorts of demands are made of them. Below are some examples of the ways in which tasks might be varied. Note that variety can be achieved both within and between these groupings.

- Different *task demands*, e.g. practice items; problem-solving; making and testing suggestions; tasks requiring imagination.
- Different *modes of working*, e.g. reading; writing; practical work; physical activity; discussion; role-play.
- Different *sources of stimulus*, e.g. questions posed by the teacher – open as well as closed; explanations by the teacher; worksheets; stories; objects; living things; audio and video tapes; overhead projector; visiting speakers.
- Different *opportunities for pupil interaction*, e.g. whole-class; collaborative working in pairs and small groups.
- Different *demands on pupils' initiative*, e.g. tasks which are highly structured by the teacher; somewhat structured tasks; tasks which leave much room for choice.
- Different *audiences for whom work is produced*, e.g. the teacher; the class; school; assembly; a display in the corridor/entrance area; parents.

In some classrooms, variety is provided through the provision of diverse activities all going on at once, with children working at those they have chosen themselves. However, another finding of the Mortimore survey was that behaviour was better in classes where not more than two or three different curriculum areas were available to the children at any one time. This enabled the teacher to give more time to teaching, focusing on the topic and key concepts rather than on organisational matters. It also facilitated whole class discussion, listening skills and the sharing of ideas. This does not mean that teachers should invariably avoid multi-task lessons; but, it does suggest that that special skills in organisation are needed. The important question to ask is: 'Does my decision about diverse activities allow me to spend as much of my time as possible in a teaching role?' The Director of Inspection at OFSTED recently pointed out that in too many classrooms visited, 'the high work rate of teachers often stood in sharp contrast to the low work rate of the pupils' (Rose, 1995, p.19). Teaching is not achieved if you are preoccupied with managerial concerns.

Many teachers find that they can organise variety in group work more successfully if all groups are working on one area of the curriculum (say, mathematics), but each group is working on a different set of tasks matched to the interests or level of achievement of the group members. In this way, the curriculum is differentiated to address the needs of different pupils, though the teacher may well begin by briefing the whole class. The teacher can then focus her teaching by sitting down with one particular group for, say, a quarter of an hour, while maintaining light supervision over the others. She then moves on to another group.

2   *Have the necessary materials been identified and easy access arranged?*

Purposefulness in the classroom presupposes that children have ready access to the materials they need. Some classrooms are divided into resource or activity areas which reduces dependence on the teacher. There might be a writing area, a book corner, an art and craft section, a maths section, and so on. The children are then trained to locate (and replace) the resources they need, thus contributing to their independent learning skills. But for lessons when the whole class is engaged in the same sort of activity, the key materials are best set out on the children's tables before the class arrives. Alternatively, a resource table can be placed in a central position.

If the teacher has to spend time giving out materials, or if children are needing to cross the room to get what they want, opportunity for misbehaviour is created. Having everything ready and easily accessible helps to generate the right mood by providing a work-centred environment from the start and focusing children's attention on the activity as soon as they enter the room.

3   *Are the starts of lessons positive and work-focused?*

The first ten minutes of a lesson are all-important in achieving an appropriate classroom ethos. At the beginning of the morning and afternoon, a class teacher must often attend to administrative tasks – calling the register, accounting for absentees, asking about missing homework, dealing with individual problems, collecting money, and so on. But if some administrative matters can be dealt with later in the lesson when the class is working, the beginning of the lesson can then be more work-focused and get off to a quick start. Where this is not possible, many teachers find that it helps to have a well-understood procedure which allows the children to be constructively occupied while they are waiting.

If lesson beginnings should be characterised by a focus on work, so also should they be characterised by respectful relationships. By this is meant that pupils are made to feel valued by you, and you help them to value each other. We all need to feel that we matter: good teachers seize opportunities to get to know children through friendly chats both inside and outside the classroom. For instance, they find out about each child's likes and dislikes, hobbies and pastimes, skills and interests, family and pets. Such is the importance of doing this that the matter should not be simply left to chance: it needs to be part of your planning.

Here is an example of the way one teacher of a junior class ensures that she acknowledges the children's individuality, though in an almost incidental manner:

> As the children come into the room at the start of a session, I like to greet some by name – different children each time – and I try to follow up something they have previously mentioned to me. This morning, for instance, I was able to ask one child about her new baby brother, and I asked another how she got on at her athletic club yesterday. This afternoon, I asked a boy how he was feeling after an accident in the playground that morning. If somebody has done something special, I might tell the class so that their effort gets public recognition. But sometimes it's a quiet word that is needed. For example, there's one girl who's not happy with her step-mum and gets upset when she hasn't had a telephone call from her real mum who has left home. I also make a point of passing on the favourable remarks which other teachers make about individuals or the class.

For the period following playtime, there needs to be a procedure for generating an atmosphere of calm to dissipate over-excitement, tensions, and anxieties which the children bring in from the playground. Here is what one infant teacher says she does for the start of sessions:

> They come back chatting and excited with perhaps one or two tearful because something unpleasant has occurred in the playground. So we decided that after play they should come in and sit quietly on the carpet. We're together then as a group. I chat about personal matters, perhaps asking if they've had a nice playtime, and trying to calm anyone who has been upset by what another child has said or done. Then I remind them what we were doing before play, and we discuss the activities we are going to do now. This gives everyone a chance to breathe, and we all know where we are.

Lastly, it is important to begin lessons on a positive note whenever possible. With all that teachers have to do and the tensions that can arise in school, it is only too easy to start off by saying something negative. But it is worth while trying to generate a positive ethos at the *start* of a session by making yourself say something favourable about the achievements of one or more individuals or the class as a whole – perhaps referring back to something the day before or in the previous lesson, or mentioning some accomplishment of an individual that you have recently learned (see also p.45).

4 *Has thought been given to the most effective way of supporting children while they are working?*

An important aspect of generating purposefulness is to ensure that optimum conditions are created for supporting pupils in their work. In the comments on Question 1 in this section, we talked about providing support through the effective organisation of group work. Here, we are concerned with the situation when children are working individually and the teachers is trying to give individual support.

In some classrooms the teacher visits children at the tables, supervising, marking and responding to those who have their hands raised. In other classrooms the teacher deals with individuals who queue at her desk. A compromise between the 'Queue at my desk' and 'Raise your hand if you want help' patterns of working involves the teacher attending to individuals in a mobile queue as she circulates to supervise the rest of the class. What is the evidence about the efficacy of these different arrangements?

In an observational study involving 20 infant classes, West (1990) found that on average 2.67 children were waiting for assistance at any time, and that the average waiting time was 84 seconds; there were no sex differences. However, where the 'Queue at my desk' system was operating, children waited less than half the time than children in the 'Raise your hand if you want help' classes – *but* the children were more engaged in their work in the latter situation. It was the mobile queue system which seemed to offer the best of both worlds – a shorter waiting time *and* higher levels of engagement in work. A difficulty about the 'Raise your hand' system is that teachers can miss children when they scan the room because some young children find it difficult to keep their hands up. On the other hand, queues have their disadvantages: they can create conditions for misbehaviour by requiring children to move out of their seat and wait with nothing to do. They may also make the teacher seem physically remote to small children when she sits behind her desk, whereas moving round the room helps to establish closeness. Furthermore, they may make it difficult for the teacher to spot the scale of misunderstandings (Bennett *et al.*, 1984) – though teachers who circulate can also miss general problems if they are preoccupied with responding to 'hands up' enquiries (West and Wheldall, 1989).

The presence of parent helpers and ancillary staff make the task of supporting children that much easier. Even so, whatever system the teacher decides to adopt, four matters remain clearly important:

- Ensure that previous instruction, the nature of the task and the resources available are such that there should be no need for lots of children to require help at once. This frees the teacher to supervise, encourage, detect difficulties and diagnose problems.
- For low-level requests such as spellings, there must be well-understood self-help procedures which allow the teacher to use her time more effectively.
- Periodically, suspend helping individuals and circulate to ensure that general misunderstandings are not going undetected.

- Consider reducing the amount of time in which the whole class engages in individual tasks and instead make greater use of the arrangement where the teacher sits down and and stays with one group of children for a period of time, while scanning the class at intervals to ensure the other children are on-task. Bennett *et al.* (1984) argue that this style of classroom organisation represents the most efficient use of the teacher's time, allowing more opportunity than other modes of working for teacher-pupil and pupil-pupil interaction.

5 *Has thought been given to ways of managing critical points in the lesson?*

Critical points in lessons are those where the nature of the event makes the risk of misbehaviour high. Examples are:

- explaining what the children are going to do (a vital part of the lesson – but, if too long or not properly thought out, may lead to restlessness). Careful preparation is needed to ensure that the key ideas are clearly expressed in language the children can understand, with plenty of examples.
- putting children into groups (too much movement, or uncertainty about who is to be in what group, creates conditions for messing about)
- re-arranging furniture (clear opportunities for chaos)
- putting away materials and equipment (have you left enough time? is it clear what goes where and who is responsible for doing what?)
- dealing with children finishing (or maintaining they have) at different times (it's a safe bet that this situation will arise, so the programme of work needs to include instructions so that everyone is clear about what to do when a task is completed)
- ending the lesson (is the procedure and the timing such that the there is a positive atmosphere as the children leave the room?)
- getting an activity started (see below)
- ending one activity and beginning another (the steps in this procedure need to be well thought-out to prevent confusion – see below)

These last two points need a special comment. As regards getting an activity started, Doyle and Carter (1986), in a study of 11–year-olds, found that misbehaviour occurs most readily during the time when the activities are beginning. The mistake is to start to help individual pupils before ensuring that the class as a whole has understood what needs to be done and is able to get started. Not only is it very important to take great care over the initial instructions, but also – especially when getting to know a class – to move round the room quickly to check for problems *before* spending time with those individuals who need sustained help.

It is not surprising if restlessness and frustration develop when children are not clear about what is expected of them. Teachers at the start of their career would find it helpful to *rehearse* carefully what they want to say when introducing an activity, forestalling possible difficulties such as asking the right sort of introductory questions or getting over a complicated point.

As regards transition from one type of activity to another, noise levels and behaviour problems can easily build up during such times. It is particularly critical when pupils have to move to another part of the school, if furniture has to be put back, if paints and messy materials have to be put away, or if equipment has to be returned to a storeroom or another classroom. If, in the event, too much time is left, that can be put to good use for drawing the class together for general feedback, or for a story or some other activity that helps the children to feel members of one group.

6 *Has sufficient opportunity been provided for feedback and discussion about the pupils' work?*

It is a common fault with beginning teachers to allow children to work for so long on their own that they become restless. A class needs to be pulled together at intervals to provide feedback, to reinforce what has been learned and to provide further stimulus. An infant teacher explains her policy this way: 'When things look as if they are going to get bubbly, we sit down on the carpet together and discuss what everybody has been doing and what we should do next.' A junior class teacher adopts a similar policy: 'When the first signs of restlessness appear, I call the class together. We *share* what we've achieved and the problems we've come up against, and so become one family again.'

The survey of London junior schools (Mortimore *et al.*, 1988) found that behaviour is better in classes where the teacher sets aside time to talk about what pupils have been doing. Children need to know that what they have accomplished is appropriate, and that any difficulties they have experienced are being addressed as soon as possible. General class feedback also gives opportunity to share work and ideas and discuss follow-up tasks and homework. OFSTED comments that in the weaker classrooms visited by inspectors 'pupils rarely received the critical and supportive "feedback" and "feel-forward" they needed and were left unsure of what they had to do in order to improve' (Rose, 1995, p.19). In such circumstances, behaviour problems are virtually inevitable.

7 *Have discussion sessions been prepared so that as many pupils as possible can be actively involved?*

Good behaviour and effective learning are promoted when each individual feels a significant member of the group. One aspect of helping children to feel that they belong is to ensure that as many as possible make a contribution to class discussion. This is more likely to happen if the teacher has prepared questions very carefully, paying attention to their sequencing, the precise way each is phrased, and ensuring that children are not only asked to recall facts but also invited to suggest ideas and give opinions. This is not only educationally important but gives the less well-informed children more opportunity to respond and receive positive recognition. It is also good for the children's self-esteem to know that their views are being sought.

The manner of inviting responses is also important. It helps to:

- pause and look round before calling on a child
- name children from different parts of the room
- praise children for trying their best ('That's an interesting idea, Sean')
- ensure that the same group does not monopolise the discussion while the rest of the class feel left out, or choose to opt out
- allow children time to make a response (and to reconsider what they have said)
- give clues and re-phrase questions to help children along.

COMMUNICATING CONFIDENCE AND ENTHUSIASM

Studies of children's perceptions of classroom management strategies indicate that, in the eyes of the pupils, 'good' teachers are those who are at once firm, friendly and fair, who take an interest in individuals and show humour whilst also 'helping you to learn' and explaining things clearly (Docking, 1987; Wragg, 1993). Children feel more secure with teachers who manage to be authoritative yet not authoritarian, assertive and dominant without being domineering, decisive but also willing to be flexible. In these respects, the use of both verbal and non-verbal language is all-important.

To achieve the status of authority with a class, it is necessary for the teacher

---

**Checklist 2.3
Communicating confidence and enthusiasm**

✓ Prepare the way you will formulate essential instructions and explanations.
✓ Project your voice, but avoid shouting.
✓ Practice modulating your voice to convey interest, warmth and confidence.
✓ Develop strategies for gaining everyone's attention.
✓ Be sensitive to the messages conveyed in your posture, expression, eye contact and head movements.

to communicate confidence. With some teachers, classroom management suffers from conflicting and paradoxical communication. One message is carried by the words and another by the tone of voice, facial expression or posture. To give the impression of assurance, it is important that uncertainty is not betrayed in one's manner, expression or style. Observations recorded in the Leverhulme Study on primary teaching skills (Wragg, 1993) illustrate how one of the major differences between students and experienced teachers is the ways in which some student teachers betray their lack of confidence, one even standing on a chair in a final attempt to get silence.

Use of voice

The intonation and pace of a teacher's speech is obviously important in conveying her confidence, eliciting attention and stimulating interest and enthusiasm. Hesitant speech or constantly clearing one's throat conveys uncertainty and may leave the children confused about what they should do. Beginning teachers can help themselves by preparing essential instructions carefully so that they know just what they want to say and how to put it across. When addressing the class, the voice needs to be *projected, but without shouting*. Maintaining a loud voice signals the message 'I'm not really in control of this situation'. At the same time, *modulating* the voice helps to convey the point and maintain interest. It pays off to use a tape-recorder to listen to oneself addressing the class: does the voice sound apologetic, or whiny, or timid, or sarcastic, or aggressive? Has the voice a little bit of fun in it, or is it deadpan and humourless? The recorder can then be used to practise modulating the voice so that it conveys interest, warmth and confidence.

An important aspect of voice control relates to times when it is necessary to gain everybody's attention. A common experience for beginning teachers is to find themselves shouting 'Be quiet!' and, on gaining little response, continuing to raise their voice whilst becoming increasingly agitated. Unfortunately, the more they nag, the less the children take them seriously, and instead find the spectacle great entertainment! How can this predicament be avoided?

One strategy is to pre-empt the problem by agreeing a standard phrase or signal which the class understands to mean that everyone must stop and look towards the teacher, turning their chairs if necessary. Children sometimes show remarkable ingenuity in suggesting appropriate signals for the teacher to use when calling the class to attention, but a simple announcement such as 'Will everybody listen' or 'Stop and look this way' would do. 'Class four, pay attention' is too impersonal and peremptory except for extreme situations.

If the class does not respond to a request to listen, it is often effective to direct the remark to one or two named individuals: 'Peter, I would like you to look this way, please. [Pause and look to another individual.] And you, Sharon, I want you to put that away so that we can begin. [Pause and scan the room.] Right, now, everybody, listen carefully so you know what to do.'

A similar strategy which can often be even more effective is to make a *positive* statement about a particular individual or group. A second year junior teacher was recently observed gaining total silence in a rather rowdy classroom by fixing her gaze on the group of the better-behaved children and saying, 'My goodness! *That* table is sitting up really nicely!'

Posture

The way teachers hold themselves says a lot about their confidence and how they feel about their status in the room. In a helpfully illustrated study of teachers' body language and children's responses to it, Neill and Caswell (1993) point out that uncertainty can be communicated if teachers avoid the gaze of the class, perhaps looking down at their lesson notes or what they have written on the board. This compounds the situation because it also suggests a lack of interest in the pupils. Fumbling with one's clothes or objects, pacing about, swaying from side to side, or making grooming movements to clothes or head, also convey lack of confidence. Standing with elbows akimbo can look threatening; according to Neill and Caswell, children often regard it as as sign of irritation or impatience – though for that reason it can be effective if reserved for quietening a noisy class. Leaning sideways on the desk supported by one hand with the other hand on hip also signals threat, though many children evidently see the teacher as calm. Although we 'hold ourselves' when we want to reassure ourselves, perhaps grasping the middle of one arm with the other, such body-cross positions tend to communicate tension. However, as the same writers point out, the practice of folding one's arms carries less danger of this and many people just find it comfortable.

As we know from everyday experience, we can *make* ourselves more confident by acting *as if* we are confident. The advice adults often give to children to 'take a deep breath and stand up straight' is an example of this. When addressing the whole class, it is usually best to stand relaxed but erect with limbs placed evenly; hands can be placed loosely by the side, but can be used to great effect in gestures to reinforce the meaning of what is being said, to 'punctuate' explanations and accounts, and to emphasise points. Neill and Caswell point out that leaning forward communicates greater involvement, more friendliness and more interest in the children, as well as demonstrating you're in control. Confidence can also be expressed through the position the teacher takes. Moving into the group (as distinct from pacing about) helps to reduce social distance whilst also demonstrating that there are no no-go areas.

When helping individuals, positive interaction is more easily attainable if the teacher avoids standing behind or above the child, but instead squats or draws up a chair and sits by the child; eye contact can then be made as both are on the same level.

Facial expression, eye contact and head movements

Of all aspects of body language, smiling and maintaining eye contact are perhaps the most important, especially for conveying enthusiasm and interest. Neill (1989) found that while children of all ages regard teachers who smile as friendly, cheerful and interesting, and those who frown as unfriendly, bad-tempered and boring, younger children are particularly influenced by these facial expressions.

Successful relationships depend upon knowing how the other person is reacting, and for this we depend upon semantic signals given by the eyes, facial expression and head movements. By nodding, leaning the head forward and perhaps at a slight angle, smiling and maintaining eye contact while a child is speaking, a teacher helps to reassure and convey the message that she is following what is being said, has regard for the child and wants to be helpful. When addressing the whole class or talking to a group, it is also important to look directly and fairly intently at the children, focusing on different parts of the room and different individuals in turn. (Next time you see politicians addressing a large gathering, see if you can spot them using a 'sincerity machine', whereby they read their script as it is scrolled on transparent plates but unseen by the audience: because the points are revealed alternately on plates placed at each side, they are forced to turn their head from one side to the other and so appear to be scanning their audience.)

When a child is not paying attention, it often helps to settle your gaze on the culprit for a while whilst you continue talking; this saves interrupting yourself to reprimand, and thus helps to maintain the lesson's momentum. When pupils are responding, averting your gaze by glancing downwards or away will give the appearance of disinterestedness; it is generally better to try to maintain eye contact whilst also occasionally scanning the class to ensure everybody is listening. If you really want to signal dominance, then, according to Neill and Caswell (1993), the posture to adopt is a raised chin, direct stare and slightly raised eyebrows.

ENGENDERING WORK INVOLVEMENT

As we saw earlier, better-behaved classes tend to be those in which the teacher generates a work-centred atmosphere. In his seminal work on teachers' classroom management skills, Jacob Kounin (1970) identified a number of strategies which help to keep children 'on task'. These he called 'withitness', 'overlapping', 'alerting and accountability cues', 'smoothness' and 'momentum'.

A teacher displays *withitness*, or vigilance, by conveying the impression that she has eyes at the back of her head. Beginning teachers especially can sometimes be so engrossed in helping a group or individual that they fail to notice what is going on somewhere else in the room. Noise levels and misbehaviour are then allowed to develop, and the teacher is alarmed to find herself scolding and shouting, yet unsure on whom to pin the blame.

When talking to an individual or group, it is therefore essential to take up a position so that as much of the room as possible comes within one's field of vision, and then to glance up and scan the class quickly at intervals. If it is known that the teacher does this, the children will be less likely to misbehave since the chances of detection are high. For any misbehaviour which is occurring, the teacher is then not only well-placed to identify the culprit correctly but to intervene before the situation escalates.

A teacher who has developed the skill of *overlapping*, is able to deal with two matters at the same time. For instance, while hearing a child read she might look up to deal with a query briefly, or unfussily coax another pupil back to work.

Alerting cues are signals to keep everyone involved. For instance, the teacher might preface a question by asking 'Now I wonder who can give a good answer to this question?' or 'I'd really like to hear your opinion about something. It is this:…', and then pause to look round, acknowledging with a smile those whose hands go up, before asking someone to respond.

Accountability cues entail periodic checks on progress by making public requests to individuals or groups to remind them of their responsibilities, but without being bossy. Thus a teacher might say, 'Now Darren, could you just hold your work up so I can see how much you've done … good', or 'Tracy, I think you should now be helping Karen with the class newspaper', or 'We're going to stop in five minutes so that we can hear the ideas from different groups'. Keeping children accountable for their performance is an integral part of effective teaching. If overdone, children feel rushed and coerced; but if carried out gently and in good humour, the children benefit by being given regular reminders about what is expected of them. And, as OFSTED inspectors are constantly reminding us, conveying high but realistic expectations is one of the hallmarks of securing high standards of work and behaviour, yet it apparently is a principle which many teachers fail to implement.

Smoothness and *momentum* are about keeping up the flow of activity. Certain sorts of teacher actions interrupt the pace of the lesson and leave children confused or frustrated. The main ones, for each of which Kounin supplied a picturesque label, are as follows:

> *Thrusts*: An insensitive 'bursting in' on an activity with a peremptory order or question without any regard for what the individual or group is doing.
> *Dangles*: Starting one activity and leaving it 'dangling in mid-air' by an intrusive

question about another matter, e.g. beginning to read a story and then stopping to ask why a child is absent, or telling off a child about a minor matter whilst trying to explain a tricky point.

Flip-flops: Going back to an activity which has only just been stopped, e.g. 'Right, put away you maths books now. We're going to have a story. Oh, I forgot to set you some homework – can you get your books out again?'

Overdwelling: Unnecessarily going on and on about something, e.g. nagging about not having a sharp pencil when a child is trying to concentrate on how to borrow in subtraction, or making an issue of someone not wearing the correct PE kit when the class is waiting to start an activity.

CLASSROOM LAYOUT AND PUPIL GROUPING

It used to be common for pupils to sit permanently in rows but this practice is fairly unusual in primary schools today. A survey in London found row arrangements in only 10 per cent of junior classrooms (Mortimore *et al.*, 1988). In 1967 the Plowden Report advised primary school teachers to place children in small groups around tables on the grounds that this would facilitate constructive interaction (CACE, 1967). Problem-solving discussion would be promoted, and, in the case of mixed-ability tables, low-achieving children would benefit by being seated with the higher achievers. Whether these benefits are in fact realised has been called into question by recent observation studies in classroom management. The work of Bennett *et al.* (1984) in infant classrooms and the ORACLE Study (Galton *et al.*, 1980) with juniors showed that, typically, children sit in groups but work individually. In the latter study, as many as nine out of ten teachers at no time involved children in genuine collaborative work.

So what seating arrangements are best for promoting both high work involvement and good behaviour? Could it be that one reason for the inappropriate talking and messing around, so often reported by primary teachers, is that by sitting children in groups facing each other the teacher is unwittingly creating optimum conditions for idle chatter, teasing, punching and kicking neighbours under the table (Wheldall and Glynn, 1989)? Findings from the most recent study (Hastings and Schwieso, 1994), showed that primary school children concentrated much better when they were seated in rows rather than groups, and that when in rows those children who presented the worst behaviour problems spent up to double the amount of time on their work. This is not surprising since there is less eye contact between pupils sitting in rows. Since behaviour is better, the teacher finds more opportunity to make favourable comments and so reinforce good behaviour.

In their conclusion, however, the researchers do not recommend a wholesale return to traditional rows for all lessons. Rather they argue that seating arrangements should conform to one of the following practices:

In a large classroom, the seating arrangements can vary in different parts of the room – chairs round tables for a group work area, separate study places for individual work, a free space for drama or sitting in a circle for discussion.

Where space does not allow this, then vary according to the purpose of the activity:

> Just as children get out and pack away PE equipment, so they can learn two or three basic arrangements of furniture. The time taken should be more than compensated for by increased time on task, quantity of work undertaken and, we suspect, in long-term quality of learning.
>
> (Hastings and Schwieso, 1994)

These ideas match well with the concept of *fitness for purpose*, so fervently advocated in the DFE-commissioned report on curriculum and classroom arrangements in primary schools:

> Teachers need the skills and judgement to be able to select and apply whatever organisational strategy ... is appropriate to the task in hand .... The critical notion is that of fitness for purpose. The teacher must be clear about *the goals of learning* before deciding on methods of organisation.
>
> (Alexander *et al.*, 1992, p.30, emphasis added)

So: deploy the seating arrangement which is appropriate to the nature of the activity – e.g. rows when children are working individually, tables for collaborative group work. What about whole-class discussion? Not surprisingly, one researcher found that rows were the least satisfactory for this purpose, and a *circle* was the most productive arrangement (Rosenfield *et al.*, 1985). Indeed, for trust-building activities in personal and social education, teachers often sit the children in a circle since this encourages an atmosphere of openness and facilitates eye contact (Mosley, 1994). In classrooms for infants and young juniors, the opportunity to create a family atmosphere for part of the day is helped by having a carpeted area where children can be physically close and the teacher adopt a quieter and more friendly voice.

If classroom layout needs to take account of the nature of different activities and learning styles, so does the composition of groups. Many teachers find it best to have base groups in which the children are seated according to friendships and to vary the composition of 'task groups' to suit the purpose of the activity. Permanently grouping children according to ability is likely to be divisive, however – and indeed there is evidence to suggest that it can depress low-attainers' perceptions of their competencies, encouraging both them and their teachers to set ceilings to what they can achieve (Mitman and Lash, 1988). But for some sorts of activity, ability grouping could create optimum conditions for learning (Alexander *et al.*, 1992), as could groups based on the children's interests or special skills for other sorts of activity. It also appears that mixed-sex seating produces greater work involvement and lower rates of disruption (Wheldall and Glynn, 1989).

Lastly, children like to be consulted about their room and to discuss what arrangements are the most helpful to them. As Coulby and Coulby (1990) point out, children are more likely to respect their classroom if they are involved in decisions about its layout, maintenance and the display areas since this encourages the class to accept communal ownership.

Perhaps the last words of this chapter should be those of Jacob Kounin (1970, p.145), whose pioneering study of classroom interaction led him to conclude that preventative classroom strategies are a pre-requisite for effective teaching:

> Techniques are enabling. The mastery of techniques enables one to do many different things. It makes choices possible. The possession of group management skills allows the teacher to accomplish her teaching goals – the absence of managerial skills acts as a barrier .... One might say that a mastery of group management techniques enables a teacher to be free from concern about management.

CHAPTER 3

Reinforcing Good Behaviour

> While some schools seem preoccupied with bad behaviour, others have concerted policies for raising expectations and improving standards. The schools we saw which had such positive policies ... had marginalised bad behaviour by promoting good behaviour.
>
> *Elton Report*, para.2.29

Beyond infant school, it appears that teachers are sparing in their use of praise and approval. Research evidence (e.g. Galton *et al.*, 1980; Merrett and Wheldall, 1986; Mortimore *et al.*, 1988) suggests that teachers of junior-aged children:

- spend only a minute proportion of classroom time commenting favourably on children's work and behaviour;
- praise children more for their work than their behaviour;
- criticise unwanted behaviour far more frequently than they praise good behaviour.

Indeed, in the Merrett and Wheldall study, which involved 1218 teachers in primary and middle schools, almost three out of ten teachers never praised for good behaviour at any time they were observed. Evidence of this led the Elton Committee to comment: 'We are left with the disturbing impression that in some schools a pupil can only get attention in one or other of two ways – by working well or by behaving badly' (para. 4.48).

Why is praise not given more frequently, especially for behaviour? Perhaps teachers assume children 'ought' to behave well, and that good conduct does not therefore 'deserve' to be praised. Merrett and Wheldall (1986) suggest that teachers probably find it reinforcing to correct unacceptable behaviour, partly because they like to think they are successful in detecting it and partly because their reprimands may have a favourable short-term impact. The Canters (1992) argue that reprimanding is a reflection of teachers' underlying fear that they will lose control of the class. When order is threatened, teachers reprimand in an attempt to lower their anxiety levels; but when pupils behave well and anxiety levels are lower, there is no feeling of urgency to do something immediately, so praise takes a back seat.

In the Mortimore study cited above, a few teachers of older juniors expressed the view that giving praise generously could lead to 'inflation' and be devalued by pupils. Whilst recognising an element of truth in this sentiment, the researchers concluded from their many hours of observation that teachers could afford to praise much more and to criticise much less. So should teachers try to overcome their natural tendencies to reprimand more for the behaviour they don't want than to praise for the behaviour they do?

Attend any course on behaviour management nowadays and praise will be found to be a central strategy. It is integral to Lee Canter's 'Assertive Discipline', which is now gaining some currency in this country. In this strategy, what Canter refers to as 'positive recognition' is 'the key to motivating students to succeed':

> What is the easiest way to motivate students? Praise. The most effective? Praise. What positive recognition can you give to your students at any time? Under all circumstances? Praise.
>
> (Canter and Canter, 1992, p.62).

For the Canters, praise creates a positive atmosphere in the classroom, helps to maintain appropriate behaviour, reduces behaviour problems, increases children's self-esteem and helps the teacher to establish positive relationships with the pupils. It should therefore be the most active part of a teacher's classroom discipline plan. In an intensive if small-scale study examining the effects of praise as carried out in an Assertive Discipline programme in three primary schools, the teachers' greater use of positive recognition increased the levels of children's on-task behaviour (Ferguson and Houghton, 1992). It also reduced the number of negative remarks directed towards the class – probably because the teacher's attention was now more focused on behaviour that warranted praise than that which might have merited reprimand.

This is typical of findings from studies into the effects of increasing teachers' use of praise. Yet it would be wrong to conclude that all a teacher needs to do is to praise wanted behaviour and ignore unwanted behaviour. First of all, it is important not to use praise as a substitute for investigating the factors that are responsible for unwanted behaviour: simply praising a child for good behaviour when learning problems underlie much unwanted behaviour is to abdicate responsibility for ensuring that the teaching arrangements are meeting the child's curriculum needs. Secondly, according to Brophy (1981), it is just as well that many teachers refrain from praising since praise is frequently ineffective and even counter-productive. The dangers are most likely when teachers praise just for encouragement, or when they praise in too general a way without specifying what the praise is for. There is no doubt, however, as Brophy himself shows, that a *discriminating* use of praise can have a potent effect on children's motivation to work better and behave well. It is therefore important for teachers to be sensitive to the *conditions* in which praise is most likely to be effective. It is to this problem that we now turn.

USING PRAISE EFFECTIVELY

If praise does not always 'work', what is it that teachers need to do to make optimal use of praise? This is not an easy question to answer because the evidence from research is often equivocal. The age of the child, whether the recipient is a boy or a girl, whether the praise is for work or conduct, and whether the teacher is in charge of the whole class or just a small group or an individual, are among the variables which make generalisations difficult. The suggestions in Checklist 3.1 and the explanations below should therefore be regarded as general guiding principles rather than tips to follow in all eventualities.

Checklist 3.1
Using praise effectively

✓ Use praise generously with infants, but be more discriminating with older children, considering alternative ways of showing your approval.
✓ 'Catch the child being good'.
✓ Give praise early in the lesson.
✓ Avoid actions which could spoil the effects of praise.
✓ Ensure that praise informs.
✓ Praise for a variety of efforts and achievements.
✓ Use praise to communicate the message 'Your efforts are paying off'.
✓ Relay favourable remarks.
✓ Be genuine.
✓ Be sensitive to the effects of public *versus* private praise.
✓ Take account of the forms of praise and rewards that the child finds most helpful.
✓ Use praise to complement effective teaching, not to compensate for an inadequate curriculum.

The age factor

Developmental studies have shown that, up to the age of seven or eight, the desire to please adults is a powerful influence on children's behaviour. Infants seem to have an insatiable appetite for praise; it provides them with authoritative guidance and feedback as well as encouragement. Young children also seem to respond to praise particularly well when accompanied by touch – a pat on the back, perhaps, or a light tap on the shoulder – which helps convey the teacher's commendation by heightening the emotional climate (Wheldall *et al.*, 1986). This may present a dilemma for some school staff who feel that the risk of accusations of child abuse demand a 'no touching' policy: but it is a sad state of affairs when teachers cannot respond to young children's need for physical contact.

Older primary children may not take the same view about the effectiveness of direct praise. In one recent study (Harrop and Holmes, 1993), it appeared that while most teachers thought that their pupils would give a high ranking to public praise and a much weaker ranking to private praise, in fact both the boys and the girls gave both types of praise bottom rankings out of ten reward items. This is not to say that they had no time for praise, but that they judged other forms of showing approval, such as a special certificate or merit points or a favourable letter home, as helping them to work and behave better. The discrepancy between teachers' and pupils' views of praise is a matter we shall return to later.

'Catching the child being good'

Praise can be a valuable means of emphasising the importance of behaving well as distinct from not behaving badly. Yet with some children the frequency of problem behaviour may make it difficult to praise legitimately. One has therefore to *look out* for good behaviour, or, as is sometimes said, to 'catch the child being good'. This requires vigilance to avoid missing opportunities for showing approval. For example, when you ask the class to do something, scan or circulate the room and make a point of praising a child who is responding positively but who sometimes does not do so. This should create a 'ripple effect', motivating other pupils to behave likewise. 'Catching the child being good' is all the more effective when the classroom rules have been negotiated with the children and are regularly discussed because the class is then particularly sensitive to the kinds of behaviour which will earn praise.

The timing of praise

One of the reasons why many children benefit from computer programmes is that they obtain reinforcement as soon as they make a correct response. In a classroom lesson, however, children often have to wait a long time before the teacher attends to them and is in a position to express approval for their work. One study has suggested that the average amount of individual attention which a junior child receives during the course of a whole week is only 35 minutes (Galton *et al.*, 1980).

Studies which have involved teacher and pupil in a one-to-one relationship have shown that the teacher's effective use of praise has been dependent on two particular factors: praising *contingently* and *immediately* – that is, reinforcing target behaviours and only those behaviours, and doing so as soon as these are demonstrated so that the pupil associates the behaviour with the praise. However, this is not easy for teachers. As Brophy (1981, p.20) explains, 'Teachers dealing with classes of 25 or 30 students are not even going to notice all of the relevant specific behaviours that students perform, let alone to reinforce them effectively'.

It is important, therefore, to devise a strategy which takes account of classroom constraints. The aim should be to 'catch children being good', both as regards work and behaviour, *as soon as possible* in a lesson. It is sometimes tempting to begin a session in a negative manner by delivering public criticisms about behaviour or work. Children will often protest against such scolding, particularly if they think the criticism is unjustified or is typical of the teacher's management style. The class may then resort to 'teacher baiting', causing her to criticise still more. By making positive comments at the beginning of a lesson, the teacher is helping to pre-empt misbehaviour before it has a chance to build up. This strategy also encourages the children to believe that the teacher is taking a personal interest in them, and so helps to create a positive climate at the start.

A useful approach is to begin lessons by looking around the room and making positive comments on the behaviour or work of a number of individuals. The remarks could be directed towards those who are getting on with a curriculum activity, or those whose work has just been marked and which deserves approving comment, or those whom the teacher has seen behaving considerately around the school or in the playground, or those of whom positive things have been heard from other teachers or lunchtime supervisors. Then, at intervals during the lesson, time should be found to look or move around the room, finding reasons for saying something positive about the achievements and conduct of more pupils. The objective should be to include as many different pupils as possible during the course of a session.

A useful tactic is to ensure that early praise remarks include children who are complying with a specific target behaviour which has earlier been the occasion for complaint. It may be that several children have been ignoring a particular classroom rule, or that too many incidents of inconsiderate behaviour have become evident, or that too many children have taken to wandering round the room unnecessarily. Praising examples of good behaviour with precise objectives in mind is a way of dealing positively with matters of current concern. Some teachers find it productive to have special behaviour targets for weekly or fortnightly periods, focusing on a particular rule and being especially vigilant about its observance, reinforcing this through praise.

The danger of negating praise

Teachers sometimes nullify the effects of praise by mixing negative comments with their approval, or by criticising a child soon after praising. A reprimand can easily turn a positive atmosphere created by praise into a negative one. The effects of praise can also be impaired by the teacher's body language. Betraying surprise at good behaviour through facial expression is one example. Another is approving the behaviour of a child who is often troublesome and then giving a sigh of exasperation when the child starts to misbehave again.

Using praise to inform

Praise needs to be *specific* if the pupil is to learn from it. As HMI has pointed out:

> The test question to be used in all praise should be: does it identify and instance the nature of the satisfactory behaviour... The idea of what is satisfactory in school behaviour is not automatically learned or maintained but needs to be taught and supported.

(HMI, 1987, para 38)

Vague remarks like 'This is good work' or 'You're behaving well today' do little to help the pupil learn. To test the likely effectiveness of a praise remark, the question to ask is: Does it provide the recipient with feedback information? Giving praise in a general way is no more effective than giving no praise at all, according to research evidence (Kanouse *et al.*, 1981). What makes all the difference is the teacher describing exactly what it is that justifies a favourable comment. An example might be 'Well done, Mary! You've remembered the rule about working quietly so as not to disturb others', or 'Trevor, that was good the way you helped David with his sums'. The same principle applies to remarks about academic achievement and written comments on children's work. Just putting a tick and 'Good' at the bottom of a piece writing does not reinforce any particular aspect of the child's endeavours because it does not say what there is about the work that warrants your commendation.

At the same time, it is important to remember that verbal praise is not the only way of signalling that you value a child's achievement or behaviour. Constructive comment and challenging questions, if accompanied by gestures of approval such as smiles and nods, are often more motivating than simple praise. Anyone who is learning from someone else wants to feel that their progress is being taken seriously and that high standards are expected. Suppose, in discussion, a child offered an acceptable answer but you thought he or she was capable of deeper thinking. Rather than just reply 'Good – anyone else got some ideas?' your style of response might be something like this: 'That was a good answer, Tom. [Smile and maintain eye contact .] Now, I wonder if you have thought of another possibility. Just suppose ... '.

Nor is there any need to fight shy of criticising children's work provided the feedback is essentially positive and supportive. Praise used sparingly with constructive criticism (as distinct from fault-finding) is much more valuable and effective – and more likely to convey that you have respect for the child as a person – than abundant praise which lacks substance.

The scope of praise remarks

The things that children get praised for communicate messages about what teachers regard as important in life. Praise which dwells mainly on the best work in the National Curriculum core subjects, for instance, is divisive since it excludes many children by reducing the scope for legitimate praise. It is important to recognise those children who have tried hard and done their best in all kinds of activity. Equally it is important to reinforce good conduct and considerate behaviour as well as good work – though evidence suggests that children think rewards and praise more appropriate for academic work than for behaviour (Merrett and Tang, 1994).

Praising to communicate the message 'Your efforts are paying off'

In the infant stages, children seem to believe that any statement of public praise directed at a pupil is an indication of that child's ability (Nicholls, 1983). But after the age of eight or nine, children become more sophisticated in their interpretations of praise. Giving older juniors praise for easy tasks or mediocre effort, for example, can signal the massage 'I don't think you're capable of doing much better', particularly if the teacher seems to be giving praise just for encouragement (Barker and Graham, 1987).

Through the way they phrase praise remarks, teachers can modify children's beliefs about their potential. Children who experience learning or behaviour difficulties need special assurance that their efforts are worthwhile – that they're really getting somewhere and that success is within their grasp. For example, they could be encouraged by the teacher saying, 'I can see that you've tried very hard, Gail. You're really getting the hang of fractions now', or 'I'm very pleased with you, Mark. That's the third day running when you've got on with your work quietly without disturbing Jason'. The next chapter contains a more detailed discussion of the effects of teachers' remarks on children's self-perceptions.

Relaying favourable remarks

We like it when others pass on nice remarks about us, and it is important to seize opportunities to do this in school. Teachers sometimes pass on to the pupils their personal frustrations with other members of staff by saying something like 'I'm getting sick and tired of hearing how rude you are to Miss Octave in music'. Sometimes, of course, a negative remark does need to be passed on; but it helps in reinforcing considerate behaviour, and also in encouraging positive self-esteem, if the teacher relays a favourable remark about anyone who has clearly made a special effort. 'Melanie, Miss Smile in the office has been telling me how polite you were when showing a visitor around this morning', or 'Derek, Mrs Care in the playground this lunchtime said you were so helpful when Louise fell over and hurt herself' are examples.

Being genuine

Praise must be seen to be deserved. Older children are particularly sensitive about this. Praise just for encouragement will be devalued, at any rate above the infant stage, so it is important to look for something which properly merits a favourable comment.

Public or private praise?

Children at any age, but more so when they get older, vary in their response to praise, which is perhaps part of the reason why teachers often hold reservations about its efficacy. This points to the importance of noticing how individuals react to praise. Whereas infants usually enjoy being praised in front of the class or assembly, some older primary pupils are embarrassed on these occasions. Teachers need to be sensitive to this possibility, and to consider whether a quiet expression of approval or thanks might be preferable to a public announcement. One recent study certainly suggests that junior-aged children find praise more acceptable if it is given quietly (Merrett and Tang, 1994).

DIFFERENT KINDS OF REWARD AND PRAISE

Apart from praise, there are many tangible ways in which teachers, support staff and lunchtime supervisors can reinforce pupils' achievements. These include smile stickers, special badges, merit or house points, special certificates for good behaviour, extra time to spend on a favourite activity, writing parents a letter or phoning them when there is something specially commendable to say. For special achievements or progress, the Head can be asked to encourage pupils through praise or rewards. Moreover, as Jenny Mosley (1994) points out, if the school is to act as a community the children themselves can be invited to say who deserves a special reward and also to present it.

Whole-school behaviour policies need to be clear about what rewards are used in school and their hierarchy, so that an agreed and consistent approach is adopted. However, it is not just the teaching staff who need to have a say in this matter. Whatever views the staff have about which forms of praise and rewards are likely to be the most effective, these may not coincide with the children's, as was demonstrated in one recent study (Harrop and Holmes, 1993). Pupils in

Years 5 and 6 in two primary schools were presented with a list of ten rewards and asked to rank them in terms of which would help them work and behave better in school. At the same time, their teachers were asked to rank the items in the order they thought their pupils would. The results showed little relationship between the teachers' and the pupils' rankings: the teachers were poor at forecasting which rewards their pupils would think to be the most and least effective. For example, both boys and girls rated 'a special certificate' highly, but most of the teachers thought their pupils would rank this very low. Unfortunately, we are not told if the teachers subsequently changed their practices and with what effect.

With a much larger sample – almost 1800 eight to eleven year olds – Merrett and Tang (1994) found that the pupils had clear ideas about the potency of praise and rewards. Specifically, they thought that a letter sent home to parents about improved work or behaviour would be particularly effective – though since this practice is rare (letters home are more usually about bad work and behaviour), most of the children would be making a judgement without the benefit of direct experience.

These studies suggest that teachers would do well to ask their pupils just what rewards and forms of praise they find the most and least helpful, and then to test the effects of following the pupils' advice. A pragmatic approach seems called for, and the exercise in negotiating rewards should help the children to feel a greater 'ownership' of the schools' behaviour policy. Perhaps the most effective way of managing rewards is through a scheme described by Jenny Mosley (1994). This involves a weekly half-hour 'privilege time'. Children in each class suggest the privileges they would like to be offered and sign up for one of these in advance; but the privilege has to be earned, and staff can deduct privilege time from individuals who behave badly. Children who repeatedly lose privilege time can earn it back by entering into a contract with their teacher to meet target behaviours

Lastly, it is important to remember that praising children is not a substitute for inadequate teaching. There is little point in praising a child who is trying hard but finding the work difficult if the reason for that child's predicament is being set inappropriate tasks. Far from improving, the child in his frustration may respond negatively to the praise. In short, the effectiveness of praise and rewards is dependent in large measure on the appropriateness of the curriculum and teaching provision, including the 'pastoral curriculum' and the 'hidden curriculum' The next chapter is concerned with some aspects of these.

CHAPTER 4

Developing Good Behaviour

> Good behaviour has a lot to do with pupils' motivation to learn.
>
> *Elton Report*, para.4.70

As the Elton report recognised, good behaviour in school presupposes that the children want to learn and have the means to succeed. Without this, pupils will avoid work, be easily distracted and distract others, and engage in what the Elton Committee quaintly described as 'calculated idleness'. The problem of pupil motivation is therefore central to any discussion of school discipline. In this chapter, we consider four aspects of this issue which teachers need to address:

- communicating positive expectations
- promoting positive self-esteem
- promoting feelings of confidence and competence
- managing cooperative learning.

COMMUNICATING POSITIVE EXPECTATIONS

'Our evidence suggests that pupils tend to live up, or down, to teachers' expectations.' Part of the evidence for this statement from the Elton Report (para 6.3) came from the London study on junior schools (Mortimore *et al.*, 1988), which had shown that children behave more responsibly when they are asked to accept responsibility by managing their own work within clear guidelines rather than being told what to do all the time.

There is another body of research, mainly American, which shows the potency of teacher expectations in influencing the level of children's achievements and attitude to learning, and which has implications for classroom behaviour. The seminal work was published in *Pygmalion in the Classroom* by Robert Rosenthal and Lenore Jacobson (1968). This purported to demonstrate that achievements in the early primary years were influenced by the expectations which teachers held about their pupils' potential for academic growth – a phenomenon which has come to be known as the 'Pygmalion effect'. Although the design of the research came in for a good deal of criticism, numerous recent studies have confirmed that teacher expectations do have effects on children's work and behaviour.

In one study, Karen Brattesani and her colleagues (1984) tried to find answers to two questions: Did pupils gauge teachers' perceptions of them accurately? Did differences in teachers' perceptions significantly affect the pupils' achievements? The inquiries were conducted by comparing the perceptions and progress of seven- to twelve-year-olds in classrooms of contrasting ethos in urban ethnically-mixed schools. In one set of classrooms teachers showed marked differential treatment of high and low achievers; for example, teachers gave high-achieving children more opportunities to participate and more choice of activity. In the other set teachers treated all children much the same regardless of their previous attainment.

In answer to the first question, it was found that pupils in the 'high differentiation' classes did interpret teachers' differential treatment of high and low achievers in terms of the teachers' expectations of their capabilities, and that these perceptions were generally accurate. The answer to the second question was equally clear. In classrooms where pupils perceived a wide range of teacher-expectations, the difference in progress between high and low achievers was significantly more pronounced than in classrooms where teachers treated everyone similarly whatever their previous attainment. It seemed that in the 'high differentiation' classes pupils were responding to, and even exaggerating, the perceptions they believed the teachers had of them.

This research focused largely on children's reading attainment. Given that there is a well-established close association between progress in reading and social behaviour (e.g. McGee *et al.*, 1984; Mortimore *et al.*, 1988), the conclusions of this study have clear implications for motivation and classroom discipline. To encourage good behaviour as well as academic progress, it is important to hold realistic but positive expectations of all pupils.

Let us look more closely at what some teachers do which betrays their expectations of pupils' learning and behaviour potential. Research in primary classrooms by Fry (1987) and reviews by Brophy (1983) and Cooper and Tom (1984) suggest that some teachers interact more frequently and more supportively with pupils about whom they hold high expectations. They are, for example, more likely to smile, to nod their heads, to make eye-to-eye contact, to praise for right or unusual answers. They also are less likely to criticise the children for giving wrong answers, to stay with them longer when they have trouble answering a question, to show greater willingness to repeat or re-phrase questions and to give clues. By contrast, with low-expectation pupils these teachers are apt to give up more quickly before redirecting questions to more able children, or to be critical of the child's initial, struggling efforts, thus inadvertently making success more difficult and discouraging the child from trying again. According to Fry, teachers' positive communications are at a peak in January and thereafter decline, reaching a marked 'low' by the end of the spring term as their patience wears thin!

Of course, all teachers are bound to recognise that some pupils stand a greater chance of doing well than others, and much of the difference in their treatment of pupils is a perfectly appropriate response to accurate assessments of their differing learning needs. For example, teachers individualise work programmes ('differentiate the curriculum', as the jargon goes) on this basis. But this is not the real issue which is that *some teachers – but not all – treat pupils as if their differences were greater than they actually are*, and that these teachers tend more than others to maintain (if not to enhance) differences between children. By contrast, other and more effective teachers adopt a pro-active stance. They hold higher levels of expectancy about low-achievers and less well-behaved children, and they resist indulging in negative stereotyping. In so far as they do treat children differently, they do so in order to enhance their learning opportunities.

Why is it that some teachers are more prone than others to communicate low expectations to their pupils? Cooper and Tom (1984) argue that teachers who are more restrictive in their interactions with low-achieving children seem to be afraid of losing control. They are prepared to interact on friendly and supportive terms when these pupils are working alone, but they are nervous about the consequences of giving them too much freedom in general class discussion. Fearful or unhelpful remarks, or just not knowing how to handle wrong or inappropriate answers, they call upon low achievers less often, even ignoring them when their hands are up, and they criticise them more for misconduct or poor answers.

To some extent, then, the problem of teacher expectations is a problem about teachers' confidence concerning their teaching and management skills. None the less, there are measures which all teachers can take to avoid the risks of generating self-fulfilling prophesies resulting from low levels of expectancy. We now turn to discuss what some of these measures might be (see Checklist 4.1 for a summary).

Avoiding the 'Pygmalion effect'

The first three points in the checklist concern taking action to minimise the risk of forming inaccurate expectations of pupils. We are all human, and it is obviously impossible to avoid picking up unfair impressions of individual pupils. Following the work of Cooper and Tom (1984) and others, however, the following safeguards should be taken:

● *Treat children as individuals in their own right no matter what you know about their older brothers or sisters.* Don't assume, on the basis of teaching other members of the family, who presented learning or behaviour problems, that a younger sibling will have the same temperament or motivation to learn.

- *Shield yourself from the negative remarks of colleagues.* Guard against being influenced by remarks of other teachers that could lead you to form low expectations. These are often as much a function of the teachers as the pupil concerned. Conversely, ensure you are not guilty of indulging in negative staffroom gossip about 'my problem children'.
- *In reading the records of the pupils you inherit, be alert to the danger of forming and signalling low expectations as a result.* Also, in keeping pupils' records yourself, try to communicate positive expectations to succeeding teachers by including notes of effective strategies that you have used with individuals. Positive comment is also important in reports to parents to promote positive expectations in the home.
- *Avoid stereotyping on the basis of ethnicity or culture.* You may underestimate your immunity from this danger.
- *Look for evidence which refutes the negative labels which pupils have acquired.* This is all part of 'catching the child being good', discussed in the previous chapter.

Checklist 4.1
Communicating positive expectations

✓ Treat children as individuals regardless of the reputations of brothers and sisters.
✓ Guard against signalling low expectations as a result of personal or written communications.
✓ Use pupil records and staff interaction to communicate positive attributes of pupils.
✓ Be sensitive to the dangers of comparing pupils with each other.
✓ Beware of betraying low expectations in interaction with pupils who have learning difficulties.
✓ Set challenging tasks for *all* children.
✓ Be aware of phrases which label children negatively.
✓ Give support, but don't help too much!

The dangers of comparing pupils with each other

The fourth item in the checklist is about the dangers of comparing pupils. The Work of Mitman and Lash (1988) has suggested that seating children in the classroom by ability for all tasks and comparing their levels of achievement in front of the class are two of the factors which may lead low-achieving pupils to exaggerate their teachers' expectations of them. There may be times when it is sensible to group children by ability, but it is unwise to adopt this criterion for base groups. In any case, you can try the following:

- *Draw attention to progress which is relative to pupils' past levels of achievement.* This encourages low-achievers to worry less about how they are doing compared with others.
- *Give praise and rewards on the basis of individual progress and effort.* The more they are based on competition between pupils, the more differences between pupils are highlighted.

Verbal and non-verbal cues

As we saw earlier, some teachers betray their negative expectations through remarks or signals that advertise a pupil's learning difficulties and suggest that the problem lies with the child rather than the way the curriculum is organised and presented. To minimise this danger, consider the following:

- *Include questions to which low-achievers can realistically respond.* That way low as well as high achievers are involved in class discussion. However, as explained below, this does not mean that low achievers are given only simple recall questions. Their involvement is probably encouraged more if their opinions and judgements are invited.
- *Take care in the way questions are phrased.* Re-phrase if necessary to present the problem more helpfully.
- *Give all pupils time to answer.*
- *Encourage effort through your body language:* smiling, nodding, maintaining eye contact, as well as praising for appropriate answers.

The importance of challenging tasks for low as well as high achievers

It is is important to ensure that challenging tasks are given to low-achieving as well as high-achieving pupils. With pupils of whom low expectations are held, the temptation may be to set goals in terms of what is minimally acceptable rather than what is realistically achievable. This gives the pupils the impression that they are not capable of responding to challenging tasks. It is therefore important to plan activities in terms of what might be achievable rather than just what could pass as acceptable. The provision of types of work which 'stretch' pupils should not be the privilege of the higher attainers. Of course, the degree of challenge must be realistic for the individual pupil, but it should be challenging just the same.

Labelling language

This relates partly to the way in which teachers can unwittingly set up negative expectations through reprimanding remarks such as 'Why is it always Karen who keeps us waiting?' or 'Scott, I see you are messing about as usual'. When speaking to other members of staff, or even to ourselves, labelling language can also have harmful consequences. For example, the unfortunate use of the term 'problem pupil' reinforces the belief that the child will not change and so sets up a vicious circle of negative expectations (see Chapter 1). It is better, if more cumbersome, to use the expression 'pupil with behaviour problems' which does not carry the implication that the source of the difficulty is necessarily something internal to the child. The official term 'children with special needs' has the important advantage of pointing to professional responsibilities (needs must be addressed), but there is a tendency to slide into talking about 'SEN pupils'. This sounds uncomfortably like the outdated and labelling term 'ESN pupil' and draws attention to the pupil's deficiencies rather than the pupil's needs. It is, to be sure, difficult to find satisfactory terms which reduce the risk of labelling, but perhaps it is worth being a little tortuous in our everyday conversations to avoid placing pupils into 'medical' categories. In short, we need to ensure that the words we use in discussion about problem behaviour is contributing to solving the problem, not to perpetuating it.

The danger of giving too much support

When a child is finding a task difficult, there is often the temptation to step in and help too much. Of course support is needed – that is most important – but if the teacher does the work for the child the message effectively is 'I don't think you're really up to doing that on your own or to accept challenge'. The kind of support that is needed is one in which the teacher shares the child's successes, however gradual and faltering, and provides strategies to help the child become an independent learner.

ENHANCING SELF-ESTEEM

One of the ways in which human beings vary in their self-perceptions is the extent to which each 'considers himself to be capable, significant, successful, worthy' (Coopersmith, 1967, p. 5). Those who have positive self-concepts are said to be high in self-esteem, while those with negative self-concepts are low in self-esteem. Self-esteem is thus about how we evaluate our worth, or the extent to which we feel we are somebody.

Research suggests an association between school behaviour, school achievement and levels of self-esteem, but it is not clear which is the cause and which is the effect in this triangular relationship. Very likely the influences work in all directions, but it is generally accepted that low self-esteem leads to lack of confidence, anxiety, difficulty in making friends, difficulty in adjusting to school, low achievement and poor relationships with others (Kagan *et al.*, 1969). In general, how much a child will progress is greatly influenced by how well he accepts himself and expects to experience success.

The seminal work on self-esteem was conducted by Stanley Coopersmith (1967), who observed and interviewed over 1700 ten-year-old boys. Coopersmith found that levels of self-esteem were associated with styles of upbringing. Boys with high self-esteem had parents who wanted to know their sons' opinions and valued what they had to say, making them feel that they mattered and were significant as persons. By contrast, those with low self-esteem had parents who did not treat them seriously, who were inconsistent in the standards of behaviour demanded, and were either permissive or punitive in their control strategies.

However, it is now realised that, although relationships with parents are particularly important in the development of self-esteem, relationships with other significant adults also materially affect the image which children have of themselves. Through undue criticism, negative labelling and sarcasm, teachers can easily reinforce children's low self-esteem – but they can also enhance it through positive measures. Indeed, one study demonstrated that the school has a greater influence than background factors on the way children regard themselves (Mortimore *et al.*, 1988). To disregard factors which affect young children's levels of self-esteem is to deprive those children of the opportunity to develop a sense of personal control and to function at their maximum potential.

Self-esteem is clearly affected by many factors, but those in Checklist 4.2 appear to be particularly important. The ideas which follow are therefore grouped under these headings.

Checklist 4.2
Enhancing self-esteem and feelings of competence

Use a range of strategies to ensure that:
✓ everyone has frequent opportunities to succeed
✓ children have knowledge of their own successes
✓ children believe that others value them.

In interaction with children:
✓ know the criteria by which success and failure should be attributed to ability or to effort
✓ avoid an unduly competitive atmosphere
✓ remain positive and supportive when the child experiences difficulty
✓ take care over which pupils you use to demonstrate skills.

Having the opportunity to succeed

High self-esteem appears to be a consequence of successfully meeting challenges. This has a number of important implications for classroom motivation:

- *Convey the message 'This is hard, but I know you can do it'* (Purkey, 1970). As we saw in the last section, children not only need to be provided with challenging activities, they also need to know that the teacher expects them to respond successfully.
- *Be realistically challenging.* Too much practice work will lead to boredom; equally, work which is too demanding will lead to frustration. Both these situations are unproductive educationally and may lead to disruptive behaviour. What is needed is a challenge which is beyond the pupils' current levels of achievement but also within their grasp.
- *Provide challenges early and regularly.* Nothing succeeds like success. This is why it is important to present complicated activities, such as learning new concepts in mathematics, as a series of short-term manageable goals which facilitate positive and frequent feedback.
- *Cater for the range of interests and skills among class members.* Because children are motivated by challenges which they enjoy, it is important to present a variety of activities both in the classroom and through extra-curricular activities. A good range of school clubs, opportunities for participation in drama and music, displays, sports of various kinds – all these give opportunities for children to show what they can do and to develop new skills and interests. Like intelligence or creativity, self-esteem may not be a global concept, so we may have high levels with respect to some aspects of ourselves and low levels for others. Because self-esteem may vary according to the context we are in, pupils need a range of different types of environment and activity so that they have the chance to feel successful and to develop a sense of worth.
- *Provide feedback + support.* Children will be motivated by challenges if they know that assistance is available when difficulties arise. Setting aside time to talk to the class and to individuals about what they have done is a crucial element in classroom management strategy. It provides reassurance for the pupils and signals to the teacher the kind of provision which then needs to be made.
- *Involve the children in determining their immediate goals.* From research studies on learning to read, it seems that children make progress more quickly when the teacher actively involves the children in setting targets for the next step (Schunk, 1987). Presumably the children then feel more committed to the goals and believe they are achievable. We are all the more motivated to respond positively to our own challenges than to satisfy requirements

imposed upon us. So rather than just tell children every time what they must now do to make further progress, the teacher should encourage them to make suggestions about what the next step should be.

Having knowledge of your own successes

It is not enough to have the opportunity to succeed, however. We must know what constitutes success and the respects in which we have been successful. People sometimes say, 'She doesn't do justice to herself' or 'He's better than he realises', suggesting that it is possible to be successful and not really know it, or to dwell unduly on one's failures and overlook what one has done well. Young children in particular need help in identifying the kinds of things in which success should be valued, in appreciating their assets, and in monitoring their own achievements. In this way they build up a clearer self-picture and can set themselves realistic challenges.

There are a number of strategies which encourage children to reflect upon their successes and capabilities. Here are some of them:

- *Encourage each child to keep a 'Diary of Good Things'*. This idea, suggested by Gurney (1990), is a way of helping pupils to appreciate their strengths and to counter self-denigrating tendencies. Besides a diary, children can make lists of the things they are good at and revise these at intervals. As Gurney points out, less confident children who keep records of this kind are able to remind themselves of what they are good at, while teachers are provided with a useful source of material for individual and group discussion. It is important to encourage children to think in terms of their personal lives and events outside the classroom, as well as about formal school activities. These include not only clubs, hobbies, skills and talents but also personal deeds. Helping to care for a sick relative, befriending a lonely child or one who has been bullied, noting positive things about others, being calm in an emergency, cheering up your mum – all are important human achievements which deserve recognition.
- *Consider having children keep a 'Success Book'*. This is a more structured activity and also more time-consuming, but worth while especially for children low in self-esteem. The idea, described by Coulby and Coulby (1990), helps children to recognise their strengths and share their efforts. Each week time is set aside for children to monitor and evaluate their achievements on prepared sheets which list aspects of school work and social activities plus one or two items which are special for each child. As can be seen in Figure 4.1, the children rate their endeavours by drawing a star, smiley face or thumbs-down sign by each item (or it could be a smiley face, straight face and gloomy face). The teacher also finds time to talk to individuals about their evaluations so that general comments by the child

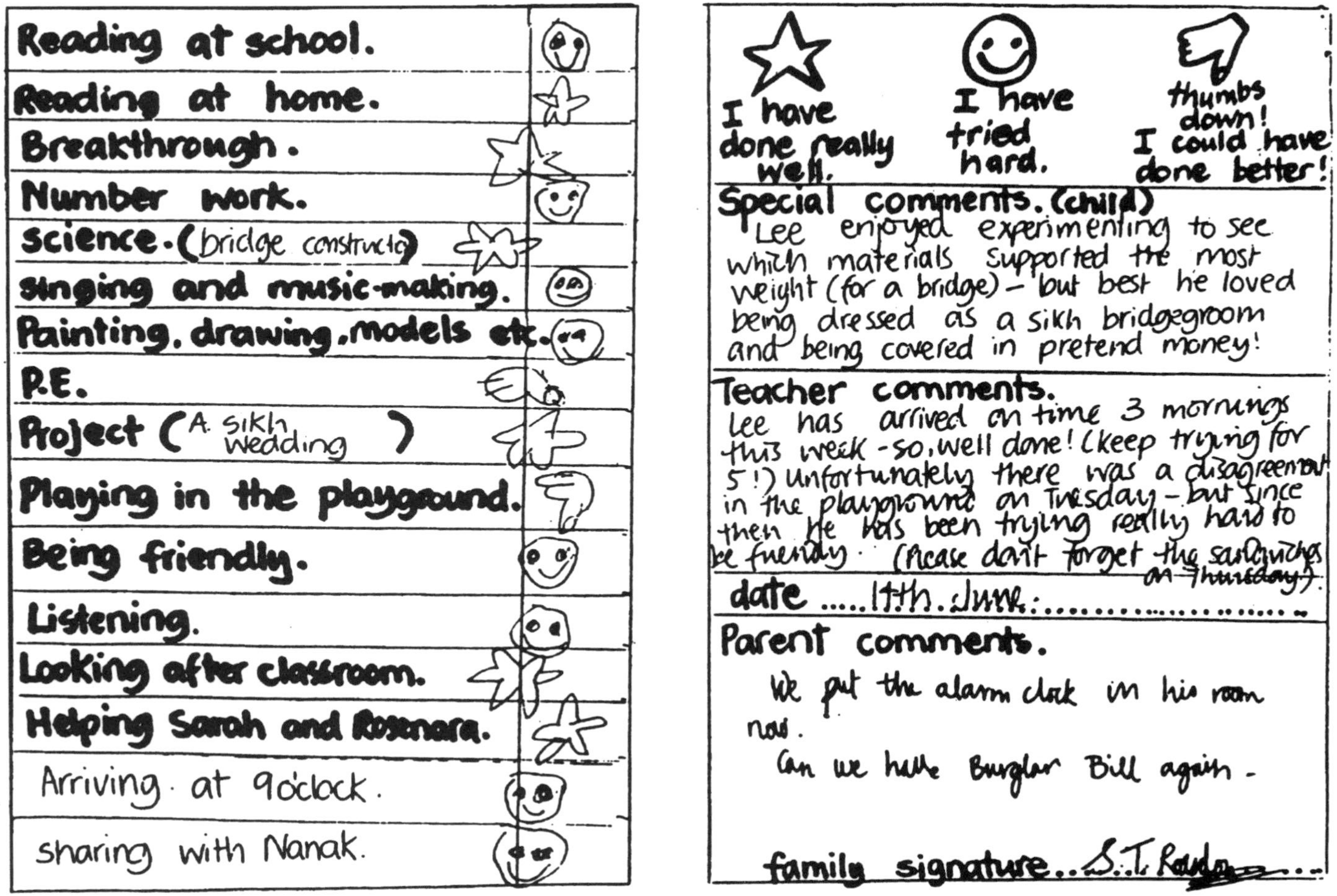

☆ I have done really well.	☺ I have tried hard.	👎 thumbs down! I could have done better!

Special comments. (child)

Lee enjoyed experimenting to see which materials supported the most weight (for a bridge) – but best he loved being dressed as a sikh bridegroom and being covered in pretend money!

Teacher comments.

Lee has arrived on time 3 mornings this week – so well done! (keep trying for 5!) Unfortunately there was a disagreement in the playground on Tuesday – but since then he has been trying really hard to be friendly. (Please don't forget the swimming on Thursday!)

date ......17th June......

Parent comments.

We put the alarm clock in his room now.

Can we have Burglar Bill again –

family signature....S.T.Rowe....

Reading at school.

Reading at home.

Breakthrough.

Number work.

Science. (bridge construct)

Singing and music-making.

Painting, drawing, models etc.

P.E.

Project (A sikh wedding)

Playing in the playground.

Being friendly.

Listening.

Looking after classroom.

Helping Sarah and Rosemara.

Arriving at 9 o'clock.

Sharing with Nanak.

Figure 4.1 A page from a 'success' book

and teacher can be added. The scheme can be extended by involving the parents, as in the example shown. Each child takes the Success Book home for parents to add their comments, thus helping to set up important triangular relationships between pupil, teacher and parent. Although time-consuming, this device gives children a framework in which to identify their successes and efforts and to indicate areas in which more encouragement and support are needed.

- *Have children make positive self-referent statements.* This is another idea presented by Gurney (1990), who found it especially useful with children who have learning difficulties. The strategy involves training children to make positive comments about what they have achieved. A pupil with difficulty in mathematics but who has made some progress, for instance, is encouraged to say to the teacher 'I did well in maths today'. The teacher then reinforces this positive self-referent statement through praise. It might be worth trying this yourself to help you believe you are making progress in spite of problems, such as teaching a good lesson on a tricky topic, coming to terms with manoeuvres for your driving test, going on the stage – any situation in which you need to give yourself a pat on the back.

Having a strong sense of identity

Teachers can help to enhance children's sense of personal identity through activities which reinforce their self-awareness and sense of uniqueness. Approaches include getting children to

- devise personal coats of arms
- draw self-portraits
- make advertisements about themselves.

As Gurney (1990) comments, these activities can generate interesting display material and create opportunities for lively discussion about individuals' personal attributes and achievements.

Believing that others value you

All of us need to feel that our individuality is respected by those who are socially significant in our lives. Young children are especially dependent upon their relationships with adults and need to feel that the teacher is taking a personal interest in them, valuing their uniqueness and not seeing them as just a member of the group. Good teachers therefore seize opportunities to get to know children through friendly chats. For instance, they discuss a child's likes and dislikes, what the child feels confident or apprehensive about, skills and interests, family and pets.

However it is also important for children to learn how to value each other.

Leech and Wooster (1986) describe a game which could be played for five or ten minutes at any convenient time during the day. You will need to have prepared a box or bag of small cards containing the names of each child in the class. To start the game, you draw two cards at random and read out the names. The first named child is then asked to make a positive statement about the second. This procedure is repeated a few more times. This idea has been taken further by Murray White (1990), who describes a strategy whereby each class chooses a 'special child' for the day. The class will have blown up balloons inside of each of which is placed a slip bearing the name of one child. The balloons are hung from the classroom ceiling, and each morning one is burst to see who is the special child for that day. The child is then presented with a sticker saying 'I'm special', and withdraws from the room while the rest of the class discuss all the nice things that can be said about their classmate. The child is then called back in to receive the compliments. This is hugely enjoyable and gives children a real boost.

Ideas such as these are a demonstration of the belief that, if the development of self-esteem is to be taken seriously, children need structured opportunities for exploring issues that affect relationships or make school life a problem for them. An invaluable framework for this is provided in *circle-time*. The purpose of circle-time is to nurture self-esteem by encouraging class members, in a safe environment, to take equal responsibility for examining issues and solving problems. The strategy should be incorporated into the main school curriculum, effectively forming an important part of the PSE programme. Because it promotes a positive school ethos and helps to promote feelings of honesty, openness, trust and belonging to the community, it has important implications for reducing unwanted behaviour and encouraging good behaviour.

The teacher joins the children sitting in a circle, preferably on chairs, and engages them in activities which relate to issues that concern them. Meetings last for about an hour and are held at regular weekly times and also whenever a particular problem arises or there is something to celebrate. Certain ground rules must first be discussed and established with the children to maximise the chances of the circle discussion running smoothly and being an enjoyable experience for everybody. This is better than imposing rules since the children then have ownership of them, but examples might be the rule that only one person speaks at a time, that everyone must listen to what others say, that circle members should address each other by name, and that everyone must be tolerant of others' awkward attempts and mistakes.

The process of helping children to value each other during circle-time can be facilitated through using various games and activities. Below are some of the main sorts of ideas for classroom circle work, but there are others too and this brief summary is no substitute for reading Bliss and Tetley (1993, 1995) or Mosley (1994), who provide numerous practical examples. Because Jenny

Mosley also believes that circle-time should be incorporated into a whole-school policy, involving not only all classes but also the teaching and support staff, mid-day supervisors and parents – indeed, the whole school community. Her book also contains ideas for staff and parent meetings. Bliss and Tetley specifically link circle-time with the moral and spiritual dimensions of the National Curriculum.

Games: to generate enjoyment, unite the class, dissipate tensions and encourage self-control and group skills. One game described by Jenny Mosley is called 'Finder of the Treasure'. Having made up a story about someone who has some treasure and placed the 'treasure' under a chair on which sits the keeper, who is blindfolded, the children place various obstacles round the chair, such as other chairs and crunched up pieces of paper. A 'finder' then has to try to reach the treasure without the knowledge of the keeper, who, when disturbed, shouts 'Stop' and points in the direction of the noise. If the keeper points accurately, another 'finder;' has a go. Afterwards, discussion ensues around general questions which the game raises, such as 'What kind of treasures or goals do we look for in life?', 'What stops us getting them?', 'How can we surmount these obstacles?'.

Rounds: a theme is selected (e.g happiness, completing the sentence 'I feel happy when …', or 'I am afraid when …'). Everyone in turn is encouraged to make a comment, all comments are acceptable, and no one may comment on what anyone else says, but anyone who doesn't want to speak can 'pass' (or contribute later in the round).

Brainstorming: to elicit suggestions. Again a topic is decided upon, but this time the circle members don't wait their turn but pour out ideas as they think of them (though still speaking one at a time). To encourage the children to be fluent in their suggestions, prioritising them for more structured discussion is left until afterwards.

Discussion: to take brainstorming a step further, so that views initially expressed freely and without evaluation are now examined and compared. It can also be facilitated through *pairwork*, whereby pairs of children discuss an issue before sharing their ideas with the whole circle.

Drama: to help pupils express feelings they would rather not verbalise, to empathise, to experiment with new behaviours.

Reflection: the circle cooperates in reflecting on an experience members have recently shared by asking what it means to them.

Other sources of practical ideas to build children's self-esteem will be found in the Further Reading section at the end of this book.

DEVELOPING FEELINGS OF CONFIDENCE AND COMPETENCE

Closely associated with the concept of self-esteem is that of competency or self-efficacy, the belief that one will succeed in an activity or task. A child's sense of competency will be affected by his or her level of self-esteem. In this section, we consider the possibility that children's motivation to engage in curriculum activities and to feel competent in them is, in part, a consequence of the way they tend to explain their successes and failures, both to themselves and to others.

Adults as well as children often attribute their successes and failures to what they assume are their inherent abilities. Thus they make remarks like 'I'm no good at sums' or 'I'm clever in gymnastics' or 'I could never understand physics'. As Schunk (1987) points out, beliefs in one's ability and competence can make a difference in how you behave. If you hold doubts about your capability to learn something or be competent in it, you will probably make little effort to improve ('What's the point?', you may say) and you'll try to avoid the activity so as not to experience failure. Those who have stronger beliefs about their competencies will not only be more satisfied in engaging in the activity but will have greater confidence about succeeding in the future. They will therefore be more motivated and willing to put in more effort. These considerations are related to a corpus of knowledge known as attribution theory, which describes the causal explanations individuals infer for their own successes and failures and those of others.

Weiner's attribution model

The work of Bernard Weiner and his colleagues has been particularly influential in relating attribution theory to educational contexts. Weiner (1979) argues that the explanations we give for our successes and failures can be classified in a number of ways. Three of these are particularly important:

1   LOCUS OF CAUSALITY

    This refers to whether we are attributing the event to something about ourselves (an internal attribution) or to something that lies outside ourselves (an external attribution). Suppose you had to deal with some kind of problem or complete a task, you might make an *internal* attribution for your success or failure by saying, for example:
    'I'm just no good at that sort of thing' (ability)
    'I tried really hard and it worked!' (effort)
    'I just didn't feel like doing it' (mood)
    'I'm a practical rather than an academic sort of person' (personality)
    'I had a headache that day' (state of health).

Alternatively, you might make an *external* attribution, such as:
'It was so hard, I'm sure no one could do it' (difficulty of task)
'He was so supportive and gave me so much encouragement' (degree of help given)
'The room was so cold and there was a road drill going outside' (conditions for working)
'I was just fortunate' (luck or chance).

2   STABILITY OVER TIME
This refers to the extent to which the factor is either enduring or subject to change. For example, ability is regarded by most people as a fairly permanent characteristic, whereas our luck or state of heath or the amount of effort we expend can go up and down quite considerably.

3   CONTROLLABILITY
This refers to the extent to which the factor can be controlled by our own volition. We can *decide* to try harder, for instance, or not to bother, but it is typically assumed that we can't will ourselves to be more intelligent.

Now, it is part of Weiner's theory that the particular cause which an individual identifies as responsible for a successful or unsuccessful event has consequences for the prospect that individual holds about future performance. Consider, for example, two children, one of whom is successful in some mathematics activity and the other unsuccessful. Both, however, attribute their experience to beliefs about their general ability, or, more specifically, to ability in mathematics. The successful one says 'I'm good at all school subjects' or 'Anything to do with numbers comes easily to me', while the other says 'I think I must be stupid' or 'I'm no good at sums'. According to Weiner, the first child will feel confident about succeeding in future maths activities because ability is generally regarded as something one 'has' and which is fairly permanent, not fluctuating from one moment to the next. For the same reason the child who has not been successful will feel resigned to failing in the future: if ability is something you've got or not got, and is a 'fixed' quantity over which one has no control, what chance is there of ever doing well? Here lie the seeds of alienation and possibly disruptive behaviour.

But suppose that, instead of referring to ability, each of these two children explain their experiences in terms of the amount of effort they have made. The successful child says 'Oh, it's because I tried really hard' and the unsuccessful one says 'Well, I didn't put much work into it'. Then, argues Weiner, *both* children have reason to be optimistic about doing well next time because effort is not just something you've got or not: it can vary from one time to the next and also (to a large extent) be controlled by the will. In short, the child who was successful can reasonably assume that, by continuing to try hard, all will be well in the future, while the child who failed can also believe that success is possible by making a bigger effort.

All this might suggest that teachers should encourage children to attribute their successes either to trying hard or to having the requisite ability, and to attribute their failures to insufficient effort but not to lack of ability. Although, as we shall see, this may be a helpful approach to the problem of pupil motivation, applying this model to primary school pupils is not a straightforward matter because Weiner's studies were with older children and adults. We must turn to more recent attributional studies involving younger children.

Recent findings with younger children

Since Weiner's work, a number of particularly interesting sorts of findings have emerged in studies involving young children. One is that primary and early secondary children use a more extensive range of attributions than Weiner allowed for. A British study by Little (1985) showed that children between five and fourteen years certainly refer a great deal to ability and effort when explaining their successes and failures, but they also refer to other factors such as whether they muck around, whether they work too fast or too slowly, and how much time they spend on an activity. Unlike adults, they apparently make little reference to the difficulty of the task or to luck.

Another finding relates to gender differences among infant children. Five-year-old boys tend to exhibit 'self-enhancing' patterns of attributions, giving internal attributions for success but not for failure (which was often ascribed to an external and uncontrollable factor such as the difficulty of the task, thus protecting their self-esteem). In contrast, girls are 'self-derogating', giving internal attributions for both successes and failures (which could induce lower self-esteem since failure is seen as a consequence of weak capability) (Burgner and Hewstone, 1993).

A third finding concerns the way children's attributional styles change as they get older. In Little's study, the five-year-olds would often explain a success simply by describing it. For example, when invited to account for the fact that one child had painted a better picture than another, a girl said 'The nice one is much nicer and the horrible one, it's much horribler'. However, as children move up the primary school, they make more attributions to specific and general competence. They now talk about 'knowing how to do sums' or 'being clever'. Most of all, they come to realise the importance of effort and taking an interest in their work: the five-year-olds seldom used effort in their explanations.

Findings about children's developing understanding of the role of ability and effort has also been noted in some American studies. Nicholls (1983), for example, found that children in the very early years of schooling assume that success, ability and effort go together. For them, people who work hard are people who are good at things and are successful, and those who do not make an effort are stupid and unsuccessful. Trying hard is thus seen as a sign of being clever, not as an independent attribute. During their early junior years, pupils come to realise that even stupid people can sometimes be successful and that clever people can fail. Ability is now seen as something separate from effort, though still not as a 'fixed' characteristic. Pupils at this age assume that by working harder they will actually get more clever. It is not until the last year of primary or the early years of secondary school that children come to adopt the prevalent adult view that no amount of effort can improve one's ability: there are limits to what one is capable of doing.

So what should teachers do?

Following Nicholls's findings, it might be tempting for the teacher of young primary children to think that it makes no difference whether she encourages her pupils to attribute their failures to lack of ability or to lack of effort, given their immature understanding of these concepts. However, Colin Rogers (1990) has argued that this conclusion would be unwarranted. For if children get into the habit of explaining personal failure in terms of a low level of ability, this may not matter very much at the time but it will have adverse effects on their beliefs about the prospects of future success when they come to regard ability as a stable factor. It is thus very important for teachers to be sensitive to children's attributional styles, even during the infant and early junior years, because these have implications for educational success later on.

The key issue for teachers concerns the extent to which they can encourage children to hold beliefs about their personal competence which will help them to remain optimistic about future success. From reviews of literature in this area (Bar-Tal, 1984; Rogers, 1987, 1990; Schunk, 1987), it seems that, while competence beliefs and attribution styles are partly dispositional and cultural matters, they are also subject to the individual's experiences of success and failure. The evidence points clearly to the fact that teachers can and do influence pupils' attributions, feelings of confidence and beliefs in their general and specific competencies. Five influencing factors seem particular important:

- *Give pupils opportunities for frequent success.* As we saw earlier, this is a matter which materially affects self-esteem. Children are more likely to judge themselves efficacious if they experience success more often than failure.The more a child experiences success, the more that child will assume that this is due to his or her own ability and not just to hard work. Conversely, the less failure is the rule, the more inclined will the child be to put lack of success down to lack of effort. Hence, once again, we see the importance of the teacher creating regular opportunities for success. This not only includes matching work to children's previous achievements, communicating positive expectations, presenting complicated material in short and manageable chunks, and providing chances for children to experience success in a variety of activities. It also means that the child should be given opportunities to explore materials and to experiment independently, and the role of the teacher here is to reinforce each successful step through remarks which specify what the child has accomplished. The more a child experiences repeated success, which in turn involves teachers and other adults in acknowledging that success, the more he or she will want to learn and to try new activities. Conversely, a child who experiences repeated failure will become hesitant about trying anything new or challenging because he is despondent about his ability to learn and expects to fail.

- *Know the situations which warrant a comment on the child's effort or the child's ability.* What teachers say to pupils about their work seems likely to influence their attributional style. From our previous discussion, it would appear that teachers should attribute successes to the child's ability ('Good, Clare, you can do it') and failure to lack of effort ('I know you can do it, Andrew, if you try'), for this should help children to feel confident about future progress. Schunk (1987) argues further that, once the pupil who has experienced failure begins to show improvement, the teacher should communicate her belief in the child's ability rather than effort. This would suggest shifting from remarks such as 'That's good. You're working really hard' to 'You're good at this now, aren't you?'. A pupil who finds it difficult to succeed and is forever told that success depends on trying hard , may wonder why so much effort is required to get anywhere and see this as a sign of low natural ability.

- *Avoid an unduly competitive atmosphere.* Classroom climate makes a big difference. An element of competition can be helpful for children's motivation, provided that the same people do not always win. The chances of success must therefore be realistic for all competitors. Rogers (1990) comments that a class in which there is a good deal of competition, such as having frequent whole-class tests, encourages the idea that both success and failure depend on a high degree of ability. It also discourages the development of intrinsic interest in classroom activities and instead encourages a fear of failure and a dependence on external rewards or sanctions. It is important to communicate the message that we don't expect all children to progress at the same rate; we do hold high expectations for children's progress, but we also allow some latitude in these. This will reassure children who, in an unduly competitive atmosphere, would give up because they have been deprived of the opportunity to gradually appreciate their own strengths.

- *Take special care to remain positive and supportive when the child has difficulty at the start.* As Sheridan (1991, p.32) wisely says: 'Ignoring a child's initial attempts to take part in an activity, or harshly assessing a child's initial efforts as inadequate, can easily dash a sensitive child's willingness to try new activities or tasks.' Through experiencing early discouragement, children can so easily learn to distrust their own abilities to solve problems and carry out activities, and they become over-dependent on others, always turning to another child or the teacher for help.
- *Take care over which pupils you use to demonstrate skills.* Teachers often make use of pupils to demonstrate skills and help those experiencing difficulty. Under optimal conditions, this can be helpful for both demonstrator and the audience: it reinforces the former's beliefs about their abilities and encourages others to believe that they can do it too. But the latter consequence cannot be taken for granted. If the demonstrator is well-known for his or her talent, pupils who are unsure of themselves may feel unable to emulate the skill of a typically confident performer (Schunk, 1987).

  Suppose during a swimming lesson the teacher wants a child to demonstrate how to dive into the pool. It would be tempting to ask the best diver, but it might be better to use a pupil who had only recently acquired the confidence to dive successfully. The same idea could be applied to other curriculum areas. The best child to demonstrate, say, subtraction, might be the one who had recently experienced difficulty but had now got the hang of it. The point is that children are likely to feel more confident about their own capabilities if they see themselves as personally similar to the child demonstrating.

MANAGING COOPERATIVE LEARNING

It is a mistake to think of personal-social development as separate from academic education. Cooperative learning is a particular case in point. Numerous research studies have shown how cooperative learning situations provide optimum conditions for promoting *both* academic *and* social objectives. In a recent review of American studies, Slavin (1992) concluded: 'The greatest strength of cooperative learning methods is the wide range of positive outcomes that has been found for them in research' (pp.239–40). Specifically, Slavin listed higher achievement, more positive inter-group relationships, greater acceptance of children with special needs, higher self-esteem, more liking for school and a greater feeling of control over one's fate in school, increase in cooperativeness and altruism, and improved concentration spans. A recent experiment with 9- to 10-year-olds in seven Australian schools demonstrated that purposeful activity and task-related interaction among the pupils are fostered more in cooperative class environments, in which pupils are encouraged to make contributions to a group goal, than in competitive or individualistic environments (Moriarty *et al.*, 1995). In this country, Neville Bennett and Elisabeth Dunne (1992) have come to similar conclusions from their own work, maintaining that cooperative learning can lead to higher work involvement, better quality work, and more 'high level' talk.

The extent to which such benefits can be realised, however, depends on a number of factors. The first relates to the kind of demands which teachers make upon pupils. With nursery children and infants, the following are among the pro-social behaviours that might constitute the teacher's objectives: sharing (for example, lending one's toys or other possessions; sharing information; asking peers for advice), drama, helping, working in pairs, taking turns, showing consideration, developing skills in taking another's perspective. In one experiment, Chambers (1993) found that very young children were not only perfectly capable of engaging in cooperative activities such as these, but that they made significantly more progress in cooperative learning in classes where the teacher made this the subject of special focus.

For older primary children, Bennett and Dunne (1992) have distinguished between three models of cooperative group work:

- In the first model, children work individually on tasks, but are asked to talk to each other about their work and help each other. The children studied were found to work quite well in this way, and the benefits were clear: 'copying' became 'sharing', while those finishing early were happy to help the others.

- In the second model, rather more demands are made on the children, who work individually on component elements of a task, so that some cooperation is essential in planning and organisation. This also was found to be generally effective, combining elements of individual work and accountability with the need to cooperate, though young children found the 'planning' part difficult.

- The third model makes the most demands on group members, who work jointly on one task for a joint outcome, so that cooperation is of paramount importance. Compared with the first two models, this one presented the most difficulties (for both the children and their teachers) in keeping everyone involved and coping with conflict – though even the youngest children tried to overcome these problems, and cooperation improved once children got used to working together. Yet, in the researchers' view, this is the model that teachers need to work hard at if they are to help pupils to develop the skills of cooperation in the most testing of circumstances.

In a recent study which examined the effects of cooperative learning in terms of this third model, Helen Cowie and her colleagues (1994) considered that such opportunities had the potential to realise three important objectives:

1   to provide children with opportunities for interaction beyond their friendship, ethnic and gender groups, at best reducing prejudice, fostering trust and helping rejected children to be accepted;

2   to put the onus on children to work together towards a common goal, encouraging communication and the sharing of information and work loads;

3   in so far as conflicts are bound to arise, to create the opportunity for the teacher to encourage conflict resolution so that cooperative endeavour can continue.

In comparing the progress of classes which engaged in cooperative group work with those that did not, this study showed a number of positive outcomes:

- Some (though not all) of the teachers came to see the value of cooperative group work, even if they were at first neutral or unenthusiastic, though they recognised the difficulties in organising it successfully.
- The majority of children (about two-thirds) grew to like cooperative group work, many appreciating its positive influence on their ability to get on and work with those outside their friendship circle. Many also became more determined to combat matters such as racial prejudice which interfered with harmonious relationships.
- Classes that undertook cooperative group work improved their perceptions of who were the victims of bullying – though victimisation did not necessarily decrease as a result.

Unfortunately, despite these successes, the study also had some failures. There was no evidence that, as a result of working cooperatively, the children liked each other more, that fewer individuals were neglected or rejected, that bullying became less of a problem, or that children acquired more positive images of other racial groups. There were, however, possible reasons why the results were disappointing. Many of the teachers were reluctant to undertake teaching arrangements which shared power with the pupils, largely because they feared losing control of the class. Indeed discipline did turn out to be a problem in some classes – though in view of the problematic behaviour which several individuals had previously presented this was not surprising. Also some teachers either did not devote much time to cooperative work or they allowed the children to work in friendship groups where they could be expected to cooperate anyway. The researchers conclude by suggesting that, while schools can achieve a great deal, cooperative group work depends upon the teachers receiving a good deal of special help and training if many of the children present behaviour problems.

All this is by no means to say that cooperative group work should be avoided. On the contrary, the objective of helping children to cooperate must be central to any school's social and educational policy. But to be successful, the teacher has to *plan* for cooperative learning experiences and *train* children in the skills of working effectively together. Preferably, this should be part of a whole-school policy so that cooperative skills can be properly developed in a consistent ethos. Just seating children round tables will obviously not guarantee genuine collaborative learning; indeed, it may (as we saw in Chapter 2) facilitate unwanted behaviour.

Checklist 4.3
Managing collaborative learning

✓ Choose tasks which take account of the children's background knowledge and experience.
✓ Provide training in working effectively as a team.
✓ It's probably best if all groups are working on the same sorts of tasks.
✓ Try to arrange for a group size of 4.
✓ Work towards a group composition which provides social challenges.
✓ Distribute high attainers amongst the groups.
✓ Take account of children's personality traits.

So what are the conditions for effective cooperative learning in primary school classrooms in which children work jointly on one task for a joint outcome? From the work of Bennett and Dunne (1992) and others (as indicated), the following conclusions can be drawn from recent studies:

- The cognitive demands made by the teacher must stimulate challenge without causing undue difficulties. The teacher needs to *choose the tasks with great care*, matching them to the children's background knowledge and experience.
- Teachers must be prepared to give children the *training opportunities* for working more effectively in groups. Here are four activities which teachers can organise to accomplish this:
  - Each group makes a poster listing between six and ten rules for working cooperatively; the groups then share their ideas (National Oracy Project, 1990).
  - Each group prepares a mural, with certain constraints imposed to make cooperation essential (e.g each child may use only one colour) (Kagan, 1989).
  - Group members individually interview members of a team (e.g. a sports team) to find out what makes for good teamwork, and share their ideas with the group (Fisher, 1993).
  - Groups members are each given an envelope containing segments of a

circle. Each person must assemble a circle, but to do so they need to exchange pieces with other members. There must be no talking, pointing, signalling with the hand, or snatching pieces from other envelopes. (Cohen, 1986)

For details of more collaborative learning training activities, see Bennett and Dunne Chapter 7 (1992) and Slavin (1990).

- Groups are more manageable and easier to monitor if *all are working on the same tasks*. The teacher's time can be used more effectively because she can more easily predict the sorts of problems that will arise. Such an arrangement also allows groups to report back to the whole class and share ideas at that level.

- A *group size of four* seems optimal for productive cooperation. Larger groups too easily divide into sub-groups and are more likely to produce a 'free rider' effect, with some individuals opting out or just going through the motions of group work.

- Friendship or choice groups may work happily, but will not make sufficient demands for the development of tolerance and patience. At least sometimes, therefore, the *composition of groups should be planned to provide greater social challenges*. Some children may then have to work with those they don't like, but that's a desirable context from time to time if children are to extend their skills in working cooperatively.

- Groups made up entirely of low or average attainers will not generally work well since its members have insufficient skills to help or challenge each other. Able children, on the other hand, seem to work well together whether in the same group or as members of mixed ability groups. However, two able children plus a low attainer can easily result in the latter being ignored. In contrast, one high attainer plus two low attainers is usually a marked success, with the more able child supplying knowledge, ideas and explanations to the others. So perhaps the best configuration is *mixed ability groups, with the high attainers distributed between them*.

- Whether to have single or mixed sex groups is a more tricky question. At the infant and early junior stages, boys and girls naturally relate well to each other, but the situation often deteriorates in the upper junior classes. Whether the position would change if older girls and boys were more often encouraged to work together is an issue on which there is insufficient evidence – but it seems sensible and desirable for teachers to try this out at least from time to time. Where mixed sex groups are organised, it will of course be necessary to ensure that the nature of the task is appealing to both boys and girls.

- Teachers should *take account of children's personality* (e.g. whether they are shy, assertive, dominant, popular) when making up groups – though it is not easy to generalise about how this can best be done.

Taking the trouble to enable pupils to feel worthy, confident, competent and ready to cooperate should reduce feelings of 'learned helplessness' or the need to 'act out' in order to compensate for a perceived inability to cope with school work or get on with others. It should also help individuals to deal with the hazards of life and to not be put off by temporary set-backs. As we have seen, these objectives are not easily realised, but they will probably be more achievable if built into the school's agreed behaviour policy (with implications for in-service training) rather than left to the initiatives of certain teachers.

CHAPTER 5

Responding to Behaviour Problems

> Punitive regimes seem to be associated with worse rather than better standards of behaviour. This does not mean that punishments are not necessary ... [but that] schools need to establish a healthy balance between punishments and rewards.
>
> *Elton Report*, para.4.47

Knowing how best to respond to unwanted behaviour is among the most difficult decisions teachers have to make. Should the child just be ignored? reprimanded? punished? counselled? given special treatment? The teacher's problem can be represented as a series of tensions:

- The child is young and immature, yet must be helped to assume greater responsibility.
- What may seem fair and just from the the teacher's perspective may not be so regarded by the offender or by other children or by the parents.
- Inappropriate behaviour must be addressed, but what if the situation develops into a confrontation?
- Does the behaviour suggest that the child deserves blame, or is it a symptom of poor social skills or some disorder which warrant special support?

In this chapter, we first consider the issues of reprimand and other general ways of correcting unwanted behaviour, before turning to the more complex subjects of managing confrontations and punishment. We then consider the kind of response that would be suitable for children who seem unresponsive to more conventional corrective strategies. Ways of responding to children who bully is discussed in the last chapter.

CORRECTING UNWANTED BEHAVIOUR

Together with punishment, the most usual strategy employed in responding to misbehaviour is reprimand. As we shall see, this sometimes creates more problems than it solves, yet its skillful use can be effective. Checklist 5.1 summarises some suggestions, which we shall now discuss.

The problems with reprimanding

Compared with approaches discussed in other chapters, this might seem to represent a negative approach to classroom management. While it sometimes suppresses unacceptable behaviour and deters others from misbehaving, it can also exacerbate behaviour problems, alienate children from schooling, induce anxiety and feelings of rejection, and even encourage truancy. A reprimanding style of classroom management can also reinforce attention-seeking behaviour by giving it public status. Regular outbursts of anger and unreasonable punishment expose all pupils, the innocent as well as the guilty, to inappropriate adult models. The aggression may then be imitated and displaced, leading to bullying and harassment.

Checklist 5.1
Effective reprimanding

✓ Use reprimands sparingly against a background of clear rules and an essentially positive classroom ethos.
✓ For some minor behaviours, consider alternatives to reprimanding such as tactical ignoring, praising others for good behaviour, or turning a reprimand into a supportive statement or question.
✓ For persistent unwanted behaviour, follow the Rules–Praise–Consequences procedure.
✓ Intervening early can avoid an escalation of the problem.
✓ Be firm, but avoid shouting.
✓ Reprimand privately when possible.
✓ Point out the wanted behaviour and re-direct attention to some feature of the work activity, giving support to learning problems.
✓ Label the act, not the person.
✓ Acknowledge the offender's feelings.
✓ Acknowledge if you are at fault.
✓ Develop procedures to deflect confrontation.
✓ Develop whole-school policies for dealing with persistent misbehaviour.

The possible adverse effects of reprimand certainly suggest that it should never be used as a principal management strategy. However, the fact that there are dangers in its misuse and over-use does not mean that it has no constructive role to play in school. Apart from its deterrent potential, it can make a contribution to children's social development by emphasising the boundaries of tolerable behaviour and by engendering feelings of culpability and the moral seriousness of social interaction. As with praise and rewards, it can be used both productively and counterproductively, its effectiveness depending on the observance of certain conditions.

Given the dilemma of needing to reprimand sometimes whilst also being aware of the possible adverse effects of this response, what conditions are likely to make reprimanding effective? The advice to use reprimands sparingly sounds like a counsel of perfection which is easier said than practised. To succeed in this approach, it is obviously essential that the kinds of preventative and positive policies discussed in the previous three chapters are being implemented since these should minimise the need for reprimanding. As was found in the Leverhulme Project on primary classrooms, telling pupils off can be counter-productive if the teacher lacks clarity about her own everyday rules. In one example, a student battled with a class as one pupil set off the alarm of his watch, another refused to work and kept on sharpening her pencil, another played with a doll and talked to four others, two boys put on sunglasses, and so on and so on. Attempts to get the children to stop these activities were manifestly unsuccessful for one clear reason: 'the limits were not being defined, so pupils kept seeking some consistent reaction to what was and was not permitted' (Wragg, 1993, p. 171).

Because reprimanding often brings out the desired response in the short term, its use can be rewarding to the teacher in reducing her anxiety level. The trouble is that classroom relationships can then easily deteriorate as the teacher slides into the habit of scolding and criticising – which in turn, of course, will make the teacher more anxious and prolong the cycle. Children who normally enjoy positive feedback, receiving recognition for their good work and behaviour, do not usually want to upset the teacher. In this situation, non-verbal reprimanding – frowning, pausing for silence, a surprised facial expression – or mild verbal correction is often sufficient. Also, when reprimanding is discriminating and relationships are generally sound, talking to the child after class will be more effective and educative.

Alternatives to reprimanding

Some teachers wonder whether it's best just to ignore misbehaviour. Many employ 'tactical ignoring' as an appropriate response to behaviours such as calling out, clowning, being silly, or sulking, where to acknowledge the child's action would be to reinforce the attention-seeking. Tactical ignoring, however, is not a passive strategy which avoids addressing the problem, but an active one which carries a positive message. For example, on tactically ignoring the child who calls out, Rogers (1994, p. 73) advises:

> Tactical ignoring can carry the message that *that* kind of behaviour is unacceptable. It gives the student a private cue. It says, in effect, 'I will answer you *when* you put your hand up'.

However, while tactical ignoring can be a useful strategy, it may not be sufficient on its own since reactions from other children will reinforce the child's efforts to seek attention. Unless the teacher feels she can train the class to ignore such behaviour, she has to combine her ignoring of the unwanted behaviour with praise for some conforming behaviour. The technique is to praise another child who is displaying the behaviour wanted, especially if that child is sitting near the culprit. Where possible, it is best to choose a pupil with whom the offender can identify, that is one whose behaviour is sometimes similar to the offender's or one whom you know the offender admires. In these circumstances, the desired behaviour is more likely to be imitated. This action should then be followed by praising the child who has been disruptive as soon as there are signs of improvement, thus reinforcing the better behaviour.

Another alternative to reprimanding is to make a positive supportive remark. Take the command 'Stop mucking around and get on with your work!' This is often ineffective because it imputes bad motives before the facts are examined and it signals unreasonably that the teacher's support is conditional upon the pupil's improved behaviour. A question such as 'Bill, how are you getting on with that maths?' or the statement 'Sandra, I see you have a problem – I'll come over and help you in a moment' should be more effective since they are supportive and indicate the teacher's recognition that the unwanted behaviour may be arising from difficulty with the work.

Effective reprimanding

A development of the strategy just described is known as Rule-Praise-Consequences (RPC). You refer to something that the class has agreed, such as 'Remember the rule we made about working quietly', or say something like 'Susan, when you remember to put up your hand, I'll attend to you'. Then find reason to praise the rest of the class or group, showing approval for behaviour elsewhere in the classroom. If this does not work, the consequences will need to be spelt out as well as the rule: 'Susan, I am giving you a warning. The rule we agreed was to work quietly. If you do not, I shall have to move you to the front on your own'. Children do respect teachers who are prepared to punish, provided it is not habitual or humiliating and the sanction is perceived as reasonable and deserved. Remember then to look for improvement in the offender's behaviour so that you can seize the opportunity to reinforce it through praise as soon as the opportunity arises. If the unwanted behaviour persists, proceed to the sanction to separate the child. Do not reissue the warning since this may be perceived as an idle threat.

The timing of a reprimand affects its impact. Telling a child off when the unacceptable behaviour has been allowed to build up may make the child feel guilty, but it will not have the same inhibitory effects as a reprimand which nips the bad conduct in the bud (Aronfreed, 1976). If the misbehaviour is minor but repetitive, it is often effective to tactically ignore it at first, keeping an eye open in case of further trouble. In that event, the reprimand will have greater impact if delivered as the child starts to misbehave again since it will then be associated in the child's mind with the temptation to misbehave rather than with the enjoyment of misbehaving.

The manner of reprimanding is equally important. In one piece of recent research which asked junior school children to respond to a set of choices, Merrett and Tang (1994) found that pupils considered public reprimand to be more effective if delivered loudly so that everyone can hear. However, this finding has to be interpreted alongside other evidence. Comments by children in another piece of research (Cullingford, 1995) suggested that shouting or maintaining a loud voice in order to control children is unproductive and stressful. In this study, children were invited to comment on good and bad teaching styles during a series of semi-structured interviews. One kind of comment which emerged prominently was a definite distaste for teachers who shout, as the following examples demonstrate:

> 'It upsets me when he shouts' (girl).
> 'I get kind of very nervous and when he shouts I'm sort of edgy and then I make mistakes' (boy).
> 'Anything we do – every peek – he shouts at another person that's right near you. It can be ... well, I know I am a bit silly now...but a bit scary. You dunno what he's going to do ... I put my head down and prayed' (boy).

As the researcher remarks, some teachers create conditions whereby it is impossible to work or concentrate, so that children's natural attempts to please the teacher are constantly undermined.

In a classic study of classroom behaviour (O'Leary and O'Leary, 1977), some teachers were asked to reprimand softly, going up to offenders so that only they could hear. Behaviour in the classroom improved. The teachers were then asked to return to their customary loud reprimands. The behaviour worsened. The researchers concluded that ideally teachers should use soft reprimands most of the time. Occasional loud reprimands, if needed, will then be all the more effective. Most of us can vouch for the claim that the intensity of communication is affected by personal distance, so that people in general are more likely to respond to praise or criticism delivered as you approach them closely (Neill and Caswell, 1993).

Reprimanding by shouting is unprofessional for a number if reasons:

- It disrupts the work of the class and induces an unsettled, tense atmosphere.
- It sets an example for the very kind of behaviour that is not wanted, the teacher effectively teaching children to raise their voice when things don't go their way.
- It encourages disruptive behaviour in those children who yearn for more adult attention but have difficulty in gaining it by socially acceptable means. They find that playing up in class pays off by making the teacher take notice

of them, but of course it is not the kind of notice that responds satisfactorily to their basic needs.

- It may provide entertainment for some children who enjoy the spectacle of the teacher getting angry and upset. This not only makes it difficult for the teacher to gain respect: it also helps to maintain the unwanted behaviour. Being bad is being somebody.
- It prevents the offender from thinking clearly and attending to the message that the reprimand is meant to convey. With young, less able and anxious children in particular, the teacher shouting simply makes the culprit confused and upset, and is therefore of no educative value and of doubtful use as a deterrent.

If reprimands should generally be delivered quietly, in work situations they should also be given in conjunction with supportive comments. It is just unhelpful to tell a pupil off for, say, not trying hard enough if no attempt is made to find out if there is problem and to give guidance. One strategy is to move towards the pupil, quietly name him or her, and softly but firmly deliver the reprimand. At the same time, be positive by pointing out the behaviour which is wanted, and then re-direct the child's attention to some feature of the work activity, lending support as necessary. This procedure helps to avoid behaviour becoming an issue and so minimises the risk of confrontation.

Another important condition for effective reprimanding is that the teacher focuses on the act, not on personality factors. This means that she should refrain from directing attention to her own power or from suggesting that the child is inherently naughty. Teachers who reprimand with authoritarian remarks like 'How many times have I told you to . . . ?' or 'When will you learn to do as you're told?' make the criticism a personal matter. Hostile or sarcastic comments such as 'Why is it always John I have to speak to?' suggest that the child is irredeemably naughty. The effect is to create feelings of alienation and to set up expectations that John will always be a nuisance.

Through her manner of reprimanding the teacher needs to convey the idea that it is the behaviour which is unacceptable, not the child as a person. After all, much inappropriate behaviour such as fighting and refusing to comply with directions are part and parcel of childhood, albeit more evident in some pupils than others. They are employed to test relationships and others' responses, or they reflect a learning difficulty or undeveloped social skill in dealing with other people. They should not necessarily be taken as a reflection of an intrinsically unpleasant personality. It may help to get over the fact that the reprimand is justified by saying something like 'That was a thoughtless thing to do', but not 'You're a thoughtless person'.

Sometimes unwanted behaviour occurs for understandable reasons. Suppose you see a child hitting another who has 'borrowed' his or her ruler. Just to issue a reprimand to the child hitting leaves the 'borrower' free of responsibility. Better to say something like: 'Ali, I know it's frustrating when people take your things. But I'm surprised at you acting like that. Now you two, what can we do to put things right?' This not only acknowledges that the offender has a grievance, but also avoids attributing bad motives and leaves the door open for relationships to be restored.

It is often tempting to deliver a reprimand when it seems as if the child has not been attending. A common situation is the child giving a wrong answer to a question when the teacher has only just finished explaining the matter. Sometimes a critical comment in such circumstances is deserved, perhaps because the teacher has recently spoken to the child about the need to pay closer attention and the child has promised to do so. But maybe the trouble could be as much yours in not explaining at a level that the child could understand. It might be tactically productive to say this even if you think your explanation was sufficient! So it is usually as well to avoid remarks such as 'No wonder you don't understand, Mary – you weren't listening'. Instead, consider: 'Perhaps I didn't explain that very well. Let me try again.'

MANAGING CONFRONTATION

Some children get up-tight when being told off, answering back, going sulky, or refusing to comply with requests. Incidents most easily occur with older primary children who have come to associate reprimand and punishment with rejection or hostility. Children who are depressed because of discord at home may appear to welcome or even seek the excitement of confrontation as a means of relieving their feelings of helplessness. Paradoxically, of course, the experience of confrontation may in turn contribute to their state of anxiety.

Confrontation may also come about with children who have not learned the social skills of apologising or of explaining circumstances to those in authority. The less articulate pupils may have difficulty in trying to relate the reasons for an incident without making it sound as if they are unwilling to accept responsibility for their actions. Children may also confront teachers as a way of compensating for poor attainment.

There is also a greater risk of confrontation with teachers whom the children sense are perpetually on the look-out for trouble, and who seem to 'have it in' for certain individuals as 'troublemakers'. Equally at risk are teachers who reprimand or impose sanctions for incidents that they have not personally witnessed and before they have verified the identity of the culprit. This may arise when a commotion is heard in the classroom or a fight breaks out in the playground or one pupil comes to complain about another. In cases like this there is a real danger of creating a legitimate grievance through telling off or punishing the wrong child, or of limiting correction to one child when others too have been at fault. The chances of such incidents are especially high when the teacher is preoccupied in helping an individual or group (or is taken up with children demanding her attention while on playground supervision) and fails to keep a roving eye.

However much a teacher may feel aggrieved by a child's behaviour, confrontation almost always damages relationships since it produces a situation in which neither teacher nor pupil is prepared to back down for fear of losing status. The best way to avoid confrontation is to create conditions in which it is least likely to occur. Hence the importance of pre-emptive and pro-active policies, such as those discussed in previous chapters, and the avoidance of shouting at children, using sarcasm, physically prodding a pupil, or insisting on implicit obedience for its own sake.

The risk of confrontation is also reduced when the teacher refuses to make an issue out of the incident there and then. An example would be a child arriving late. There is less possibility of confrontation if the teacher settles the child down quickly and deals with the reasons of lateness later in the lesson when the class is engaged in activities.

All the same, confrontations can arise even with experienced teachers who characteristically have positive relationships with the pupils. What should you do if a child answers back or is rude or abusive? The general aim should be to deal with the situation without making matters worse and damaging prospects of building up a positive relationship with the pupil. Equally, all the children in the class will benefit if the teacher sets a model for dealing non-aggressively with threatening situations. This is not easy, but there are two temptations which are worth resisting.

The first is to lose your temper or to confirm that the remark has been taken as abusive by giving it or the child a label – 'I'm not going to stand here and put up with your rudeness'. Focusing on your power or status and imputing bad motives might simply tempt the child to continue to wind the teacher up. It is much better to focus on the classroom or school rules so that you are not personalising the issue. That said, the other temptation to resist is to interrupt the lesson by spending time dealing with the situation there and then in front of the class. This allows the child to experience the reward of generating public status, and may cause further problems for the teacher in regaining class control.

It would obviously be wrong and ineffective to ignore abusive behaviour. What one needs to do is to *deflect* the confrontation and to discuss the incident privately later on. One strategy is to move towards the pupil and say calmly, 'I want to talk to you after the lesson'. Both teacher and child then have time to get control of themselves. Later in the lesson it would be appropriate to give the child positive support and encouragement, and then, when the class is dismissed, to speak about the incident – but in a calm and non-threatening way, not as a prosecutor in court. Since the child knows that the behaviour is unacceptable, making a scene about it will only confirm that you are angry and upset. The strategy is not to get on your high horse but to refer to any rule which has been broken and to make it clear that you want to understand the problem.

In short, it is important for the whole class that in a confrontational situation the teacher presents a model of calm but purposeful behaviour whilst also showing the offender that she wants relationships to be friendly and constructive. If in the event it turns out that the child has a legitimate grievance, then the correct action to take is to apologise. This sets the right example and, in the long-term, should earn respect.

PUNISHMENT

Some of the points made about reprimand, such as being sparing in its use and focusing on the unwanted features of the act rather than the disagreeable nature of the child, apply equally to punishment. Again, the timing is important: the longer it is after the event, the more difficult it is for young children to link the punishment to the offence.

Punishment in school,. however, raises further issues which require the teacher to make sensitive professional judgements. When reprimanding it is easier to appeal to the child's understanding, but the potentially educative role of punishment is less apparent. It is also harder to make amends for an unjustly severe punishment, or for punishing the wrong child, than for reprimanding a child too harshly or unfairly.

For punishment to seem fair it must operate against a background of rules and expectations which the children know and generally respect. Punishing children should be reserved for repeated offences and should not be given if it is apparent that the child is trying to improve, however slow that progress may be. The offender should first be given a clear warning in a firm, matter-of-fact way. Once the teacher has issued a warning, it is important to follow it up at the first infringement, or her authority will not be respected.

Punishment and children's moral thinking

It is often said that teachers should be consistent in their use of punishment. The Canters (1992, p.169), take up a clear position on this matter:

> Students need to learn that negative consequences are a natural outcome of behaviour. The key is not the consequences themselves, but the inevitability that they will occur each time a rule is broken or a direction not followed. Not sometimes. Not every now and then, but every single time.

Importantly, this assertion is qualified by stressing that 'limit-setting consequences ... will be ineffective unless staying within those limits is backed up by praise' (p.169), but the message about the inevitability of negative consequences for unwanted behaviour is nevertheless unambiguous.

Certainly punishment will not suppress unwanted behaviour if used in an arbitrary fashion, for children then find it difficult to form a clear concept of what counts as acceptable and unacceptable conduct. Nor will it be effective if the teacher demonstrates a lack of assertiveness, avoiding punishing because she is afraid to exert her authority. On the other hand, the inflexible use of punishment which takes no account of the circumstances could be regarded by the pupils as unfair. For punishment to be respected and effective it is important that both the offender and the rest of the class perceive it as deserved. On this argument, punishment should therefore be consistent not just with respect to the nature of the act ('if you do X, then Y will follow') but also the circumstances of the act. Interestingly, the Canters later seem to retract on their decisive initial assertion on inexorable negative consequences following rule-breaking: 'Don't just blindly follow your discipline hierarchy. It is meant to guide, not control you' (p.185). This qualification is in turn supported by examples to illustrate that the teacher's professional judgement is needed to respond in the pupil's best interests, such as when behaviour is out of character or when a pupil is extremely upset.

At the same time, exercising professional judgement in the interests of fairness itself raises problems, for what an adult may regard as fair and just a child may not. According to Piaget (1932), children in their early years of schooling do not generally have the maturity to understand the justice of varying punishment according to the circumstances, such as whether the act was accidental, intentional or well-motivated, because they focus on the magnitude of the deed itself. A large but accidental misdeed is thus considered worse than a small but deliberate one. This characteristic of young children's thinking, which Piaget called 'moral realism', means that teachers who punish one child but not another for the same offence could be greeted by the cry 'It's not fair, Miss!', even though the circumstances were different.

There is no easy answer to this problem, but a number of points can be made. First of all, Piaget's evidence about young children's immature moral awareness has been largely superseded by the evidence of later better-constructed studies. The more recent research suggests that by the age of six or seven most children realise that blame and punishment are more or less deserved according to the perpetrator's intentions and motives *provided that* the situation is simply presented (Fincham, 1983). While older children are certainly more discriminating in their judgements, the younger ones can and do take account of circumstances. Indeed, as experienced teachers and parents can testify, young children often plead 'Yes, but I didn't mean it', or even 'Yes, but he made me do it', or 'Yes, but I was only trying to help'. Most primary school children from quite an early age, then, are capable of understanding that, say, Sharon should be punished for splashing paint on Tracy because she didn't like her, whereas Trevor should not be punished for splashing paint on David when his hand slipped – but the younger the child, the more teachers need to explain the different situations carefully and patiently. Indeed, this is part of their job as educators.

Secondly, the ability to make discriminating judgements about behaviour is not something that just happens as a result of growing up. It is very much dependent on the way we are treated during the course of our childhood by the significant adults in our lives. Maturity in making moral judgements develops earlier in young children who live in an environment where adults refrain from being bossy and domineering and appeal to the child's developing sense of reasoning about what is right and wrong (Kohlberg, 1968). We also know that children who experience a warm, compassionate un-punitive style of upbringing will learn earlier to empathise with other people's points of view (Hoffman, 1970; Light, 1979). All this has implications for the teacher's style of classroom management as well as for parental practices. In particular, the teacher's manner should convey the message that when children are reprimanded or punished it is not just because they have been disobedient or have frustrated the teacher (which would reinforce the young child's dependency on adult authority) but because they have disregarded the feelings and needs of others.

A third but trickier point which needs to be made here is that we often need to respond to the behaviour of children *as if* they were more mature than in fact they are. It is part of a teacher's job to help children gradually view themselves as responsible moral agents who, as such, deserve to be blamed for thoughtless or mean acts. Experiencing the unpleasantness of punishment from an adult with whom relationships are fundamentally good has an educative function in helping children to develop feelings associated with 'being responsible' and therefore subject to blame. This does not, of course, justify any sort of punishment or its regular use. But it does point to the possibility that moderate punishment has a part to play in challenging children's moral thinking, helping them them to feel accountable for what they do.

TYPES OF PUNISHMENT

Punishment, to be punishment, must be unpleasant for the offender. But some forms of unpleasantness are ruled out on the grounds that they are either ineffective or fail to treat children as persons. It would therefore be unprofessional, as well as unethical, to demean children through sarcasm or to apply derogatory labels to them.

Even given this, however, most punishments are problematic in one way or another. This is why it is so important for teachers not to rely on them, but to ensure that it is the more positive approaches, discussed in other chapters, that characterise their teaching and management styles. However, accepting the need for punishment from time to time, it is important to choose the kind which has the greatest chance of helping the child to behave better without the unfortunate side-effects listed at the beginning of this chapter. In deciding what measures to take, new teachers will also need to take account of the customary practices at the school. As far as the law is concerned, punishment administered in school must be moderate, not dictated by bad motives, is usual in the school and could be expected by the parent.

Punishments fall into two broad categories: those which deprive offenders of some aspect of their freedom, and those which inflict unpleasantness directly.

Punishing by depriving the child of freedom

Losing Privileges or Free Time

Children who misbehave in school are sometimes deprived of participating in a favoured activity or otherwise have their personal liberty restricted. The idea is to prompt offenders to reflect whether the illegitimate enjoyment derived from misbehaving is worth the cost of losing opportunities which can be legitimately enjoyed. The technique is therefore technically known as 'response cost'. Of course, the activity lost should not be a part of the statutory curriculum to which all children – including those misbehaving – are entitled. Teachers should therefore refrain from, say, depriving a child of a swimming or games lesson, or of an outing which is integral to a curriculum programme such as a museum trip related to an historical topic.

The problem here is that unless the activity is really enjoyable, having to miss it will not be a punishment. Yet if the activity is one to which the child is especially looking forward, perhaps a class outing to the sea which is extraneous to the main curriculum, the child may simply feel resentful and even try to shift the blame on to another pupil. In any case, by the time the event occurs, the circumstances of the misdemeanour could be past history. For maximum impact, a punishment should follow the offence without delay. Ideally, then, the privileges or freedom lost should be one which would otherwise be enjoyed the same day. Losing the next playtime is often quite effective for this reason.

As described in Chapter 3, by instituting a weekly half-hour 'privilege time', children not only have the opportunity to earn privileges for good behaviour but can also be deprived of privilege time for inappropriate conduct (Mosley, 1994). A further motivational feature of the system allows children who repeatedly lose privilege time to earn it back by entering into a contract with their teacher to meet target behaviours.

Detaining children after school is fraught with difficulties, especially in the case of young children who need to be accompanied home. Education Authorities and school governors may have guidelines about the use of detention and these should be given in the school prospectus. Parents must always be given adequate notice, and a teacher who does not do this can be accused of false imprisonment, though a judge may deem the circumstances to be justified (*Terrington v. Lancashire County Council*, 1986). Because it is difficult to arrange for detention after school on the same day as the offence, the punishment is often less effective than alternative, more immediate measures.

Teachers should refrain from keeping in the whole class. Piaget's (1932) main conclusion on punishment of whole groups still holds good: that even very young children regard it as unfair since the innocent members of the class are as inconvenienced as the guilty.

Segregating the Pupil

Teachers sometimes segregate misbehaving children by making them sit alone away from friends, perhaps facing a wall so that the unwanted behaviour is not reinforced by the attention of other children. The social embarrassment which this causes may be an effective deterrent both to the offender and to the class as a whole. The child is also no longer receiving attention from other children in the class who may be helping to maintain the problem behaviour. However, the punishment carries the risk of making the child feel unwanted and thus exacerbating the problem. It would be professionally irresponsible, therefore, to use this strategy in order to shelve responsibility for the child during the rest of the lesson. Rather the teacher should make clear that the offender can return to his or her seat after a specified short period of time of good behaviour (say, five minutes). When this time has elapsed, and provided the child has not continued to misbehave, the punishment should be stopped and the child asked to promise to behave acceptably. Opportunity should then be seized to praise for good behaviour or work, and so restore a positive relationship and reintegrate the child into the group. If the pupil's behaviour remains a problem, then segregation outside the room ('time out') could be the next move.

In some schools, children who keep disturbing the rest of the class and making undue demands on the teacher's time are given work to do near the head's room, in the school office or in another designated area where an adult ensures the pupil keeps quiet and completes set tasks. Of course, this again raises the risk of compounding the problem by making the child feel unwanted, but it does at least remove the pupil from the audience which is helping to maintain the disruptive behaviour and it also allows the main lesson to continue. On this argument, it is therefore not good practice to ask a child to stand outside the classroom with nothing to do because the culprit may find the experience more enjoyable than classroom work, especially if friends can be attracted through the window! Time-out procedures need to be agreed as part of a whole-school behaviour policy so that everyone (including parents) knows when and how it is to be used.

Segregating children as a punishment should not be confused with management strategies which involve moving a child to another seat where the teacher can give support more easily, or arranging for the child to work with another teacher for a short period of time in a different environment. Since the child is now getting *more* attention, such measures do not constitute punishment but alternative teaching provision to meet individual needs. Admittedly the borderline between 'support' and 'punishment' is a fuzzy one since in some circumstances the child may perceive the alternative teaching arrangement as a punitive measure, especially if ordered to move in a peremptory manner. None the less, a judgement must be made about the response that is in the child's best interests: is it punishment that is deserved? or is it structured support which is needed to enable the child to succeed and behave acceptably more easily? We return to this matter in the last two sections of this chapter.

Direct punishments

A Severe Telling-off

This is a punishment rather than just a reprimand since the intention is to inflict unpleasantness by shaming the child. As with ordinary reprimands, it is more effective if delivered privately. At best, it can get across the reprehensibility of the offence, but if the teacher shouts or makes demeaning remarks, the child may become resentful and confused about the moral message which the punishment is intended to convey. The effectiveness of telling-off is also closely related to two other factors. One is the extent to which the pupils in general disapprove of the offender's act. Hence it is important to focus 'telling off' on school and classroom rules which have commanded general consensus. The other factor is the offender's estimation of the teacher's standing with pupils in general and the degree to which that pupil could have expected similar treatment from any other member of staff. For this reason, it is necessary to establish whole-school policies which reflect the agreed position of staff on different kinds of offences and how to respond to them.

Doing Extra Tasks

Teachers sometimes make children write out lines. The fact that this exercise is meaningless may be why it is often laughed at rather than respected. It is probably better to give offenders a task that will help them to feel socially useful, such as clearing up litter or cleaning out a storeroom.

Sending the Child to the Head Teacher

This must be reserved for serious or repeated offences, otherwise the class teacher is liable to lose her position of authority in the classroom – as well as her professional status in the eyes of the head and colleagues. The nature of the behaviour for which this strategy is permitted, and the procedure to be employed, should be clear and agreed by all staff. There is also a need for a referral system, in line with the Code of Practice for children with special needs (DfE, 1994d), which gives staged support in circumstances where punishment is seen to be inappropriate or has proved ineffective:

- seeing the head or deputy, who, in consultation with the class teacher, sets targets for changing the behaviour and supportive measures such as new seating arrangements in class;
- informing parents and drawing up an individual behaviour plan (see below) which monitors and rewards progress towards improved behaviour;
- involvement of external agencies (educational psychology or welfare services).

Enlisting the Support of Parents

A letter may be written to parents, or they may be asked to come to the school. Certainly parents need to be informed about their child's behaviour problems before they become serious, but if they regard this as a punitive measure they may over-react and either become absurdly defensive or take it out on the child. It is therefore important to discuss positive management strategies with parents, not just to complain. For example, parents might be invited to enter into an agreement whereby the child's favourite activities at home – perhaps watching TV or going on an outing – are varied according to weekly scores based on the child's behaviour record at school. As the behaviour improves, the scheme is gradually phased out by extending the time before the child is rewarded. In this way the school and parents work together in developing a positive approach to the behaviour problem. For a detailed discussion on working with parents to change behaviour, see Jones and Lock (1993).

In view of all the 'ifs' and 'buts' about different types of punishment, what conclusions can be drawn? As we have seen, for maximum effectiveness punishment should be administered without delay and without humiliating the child. For moral reasons, it should be sufficiently unpleasant to prompt the child to 'think again' and act more responsibly, but not so unpleasant that the child perceives the 'punishment' as unjust and becomes alienated from the values which the school is trying to reinforce. On these criteria, of the various punishments discussed, the employment of 'privilege time', losing a playtime or favourite extra-curricular activity, giving the child community tasks to do, or segregating the pupil for a short stipulated time interval, would seem to be the most appropriate measures. But whatever is decided should be part of the whole-school behaviour policy. The main suggestions about punishment are listed in Checklist 5.2.

Checklist 5.2
Considerations in developing policy on punishment

Legally:
✓ Punishment must be moderate, not dictated by bad motive, is usual in the school, and could be expected by the parents in the circumstances.
✓ In all maintained schools, corporal punishment – including slapping, throwing chalk and rough handling – is illegal; physical force may only be used to prevent damage or injury.
✓ For detention (which is best avoided), parents must be given adequate notice.
To be effective:
✓ Ensure that punishment operates against a background of rules which children know and generally respect.
✓ Reserve punishment for repeated offences after a warning.
✓ The message should be 'You have disregarded our rule and the feelings and needs of others' rather than 'You have displeased me'.
✓ Avoid punishments which humiliate.
✓ Punishment should follow the offence without delay.
✓ Pupils should be segregated within the classroom for only short, specified periods of time.
For the school's behaviour policy:
✓ Consider instituting a weekly 'privilege time' in which privileges must be earned and time can be deducted.
✓ Agree the occasions and procedures for (a) time-out, (b) referrals to the head/deputy; (c) referral systems for extra support.
✓ Parental involvement should include discussion of positive management strategies.

INDIVIDUAL BEHAVIOUR INTERVENTION PROGRAMMES

Some children have special difficulty in controlling their own behaviour. This could be linked to a work problem, such as when a child, in an effort to compensate for lack of success in coping with curriculum work, perpetually behaves unacceptably in order to gain attention. Such pupils need to be given individual programmes which have four important characteristics:

- the teacher and pupil discuss and agree on one or two *specific target behaviours*
- the programme is *carefully structured* in a series of short, graded steps so that the child can more easily experience success in learning
- progress towards the target behaviours is *carefully monitored*, preferably by the child so that self-control is encouraged
- inappropriate behaviour is ignored wherever possible while at the same time, and crucially, *improvement in behaviour is systematically reinforced* through praise and possibly a special reward.

Such programmes would be consistent with the advice given in the *Code of Practice on the Identification and Assessment of Children with Special Educational Needs* (DfE, 1994d) and the official guidance on the education of children with emotional and behavioural difficulties (DfE, 1994b). The principles are largely those derived from behavioural psychology, which involves the idea that behaviour is learned and maintained through reinforcement, and that behaviour which is not reinforced will disappear or be 'unlearned'. Aversive control techniques or, alternatively, dwelling upon underlying temperamental traits and other possible causative factors which cannot be directly observed, are regarded as unproductive. Instead, behaviourists recommend a planned intervention to change the problem behaviour by changing both the circumstances which trigger it off and the conditions which may be helping to maintain it.

The process of behavioural management begins with defining the behaviour and identifying the events surrounding it. This analysis is sometimes referred to as ABC (e.g. Wheldall and Glynn, 1989). The sequence can be represented as follows:

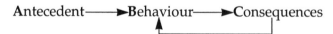

Antecedent——▶Behaviour——▶Consequences

B represents the observed behaviour. This must be described objectively and precisely, such as 'shouting to another pupil' or 'running round the classroom', and not in vague or emotive terms like 'forever being a nuisance'. **A** represents the antecedents of the behaviour. These are the events which occur immediately before the behaviour and appear to trigger it off (e.g. the teacher might announce that a particular sort of task is to be done, and a child who fears being unable to complete it behaves badly in an attempt to attract attention and 'be somebody'). More generally, antecedents are the aspects of the physical and social environment which seem to encourage the behaviour (e.g. difficult access to materials, inappropriate seating arrangements, or the absence of instructions about what to do when a task is finished). **C** represents the consequences of the behaviour. For instance, a teacher might respond to a child saying rude words by getting angry and shouting, or other children might laugh. Such responses could unwittingly help to maintain the unwanted behaviour since the child enjoys attracting the attention.

To change a child's behaviour by behavioural intervention involves changing the nature of the antecedents or the consequences or both. Thus, a child who gets restless and distracts others during individual work sessions might behave more acceptably if the antecedents were addressed by, for instance, being given more carefully graded and shorter tasks; or being seated beside a different child or alone or nearer the teacher; or being provided with more readily accessible materials. Alternatively or additionally, changing the consequences of the behaviour could help, such as avoiding styles of reprimand which elicit attention-seeking behaviour and ensuring that good work and behaviour are noticed and acknowledged.

Organising an individual behaviour plan requires careful thought and some time in preparation but the results should be rewarding not only for the child but for the teacher by seeing the child's behaviour improve. Where this does not occur, the involvement of outside agencies may be needed. Here is a series of steps that gives the general idea:

Stage 1: Determine the target behaviours
List the main behaviours you want to change, not more than two or three. *Be specific*, e.g. 'shouts at another pupil', or 'walks about the class', so that you know exactly what behaviour you want to change. Then prioritise these, putting at the top of your list the one or two you think are most amenable to change. These are your target behaviours for the current programme. Then, having decided which behaviours to address first, formulate one or two precise teaching objectives to support these, e.g. 'To teach Darren to work quietly for 20 minutes on set tasks'.

Stage 2: Establish baseline data
This stage is sometimes omitted. But if you want to evaluate your intervention programme, you will need to establish data which records the child's present attainment with respect to the behaviours you want to change; you can then later compare this with data after the intervention programme has been running for a period of time. To record the child's behaviour, keep a tally chart for, say, 30 minutes each session for four or five days. Every five minutes, you (or, more easily, another adult in the room) look at the child and record a tally if the child is demonstrating unwanted behaviour with respect to your target behaviours. At the end of the four or five days, you can then work out what percentage of time the unwanted behaviour has been evident (see Figure 5.1). Keep a note too of apparent antecedents and consequences of the target behaviours, since these could inform your strategy.

Name of child: . . . .

Examples of target behaviours
- Distracts other pupils during individual work sessions (D)
- Walks about the class during individual work sessions (W)

Recording arrangements
Every 5 minutes for 30 minutes during 3 sessions per day over 4 days.

		5 mins	10 mins	15mins	20 mins	30 mins
Day 1	Session 1	D	–	–	W	D
	Session 2	W	D	–	–	DW
	Session 3	–	W	D	W	–
Day 2	Session 1	DW	–	W	–	D
	Session 2	–	D	DW	–	D
	Session 3	–	–	DW	W	–
Day 3	Session 1	W	–	–	–	D
	Session 2	D	W	D	W	–
	Session 3	–	–	–	D	D
Day 4	Session 1	D	–	–	–	D
	Session 2	–	D	–	DW	W
	Session 3	–	–	DW	–	D

Conclusions

Distracting other pupils (D):   21 times out of 60 = 35.0%
Walking about the class (W):   18 times out of 60 = 30.0%

Figure 5.1 Example of a tally chart for recording the incidence of a child's target behaviour

Stage 3: Prepare the intervention programme

1   Choose a time when you can sit down in a quiet place to discuss your teaching goals with the child, making it clear by your manner and what you say that you are trying to offer constructive support, not to punish ('I am suggesting this because I think it will help you with your school work', not 'I'm doing this because you've behaved so badly'). You will need to ask the child why he is behaving as he is, which also gives you the opportunity to address contributory factors such as not understanding the work, or problems at home.

2   The child could then make a written contract (e.g. *'I will try hard to work quietly and not disturb others.'*). The statement should be worded simply and precisely, pointing to the behaviour wanted rather than not wanted. The

child's active participation at this stage gives him 'ownership' of the agreement.

3   Prepare the intervention programme to make the consequences of good behaviour rewarding, and immediate. Begin by assigning one or more periods each day for the programme (say, 20 minutes before play, 20 minutes after play, and 20 minutes in the afternoon). The programme should be administered in a series of steps:

- with one-to-one adult supervision
- in a small group but still with adult supervision
- in a small group without adult supervision
- in a full class lesson with light adult supervision.

4   The child is rewarded for progress through adult support, including praise. Some children make more rapid progress if they are helped to self-monitor their achievement. This is how it could be done:

- First, show the child how to keep a tally chart of his progress. Make a booklet (which the child could illustrate) containing pages of squares representing intervals of time over the part of the day when the programme is to operate. To begin with, the intervals should be short, say five minutes. A tally is placed in a square at the end of the time interval to show the target behaviour has been maintained. Although it helps if a support teacher is in the room to help with the monitoring, especially with younger children, self-monitoring should be encouraged where feasible as a sign of trust. In that case, the teacher maintains light supervision, reinforcing honest recordings through praise.
- The agreement is that after so many tally marks the child receives a reward. Initially, this could be colouring in a section of a picture or pictorial chart. This works best if it is tailor-made, depicting one of the child's main interests or pastimes. This captures the child's imagination and helps to promote self-esteem by showing respect for the child's individuality. Thus, for the child who likes animals, the picture might be of a household pet, or a pictorial chart showing a tour round a zoo. A picture can be divided into, say, five sections, or it could be a chart as in Figure 5.2. Make several copies, or a series of pictures. Each time all sections of the picture or chart are coloured, the child can receive a further reward, such as praise from the head teacher, a certificate for good behaviour, engagement in a favoured activity for part of an afternoon, or writing a letter to the parent/guardian.

The monitoring system can be adapted to suite particular purposes, including the promotion of more acceptable behaviour outside the classroom.

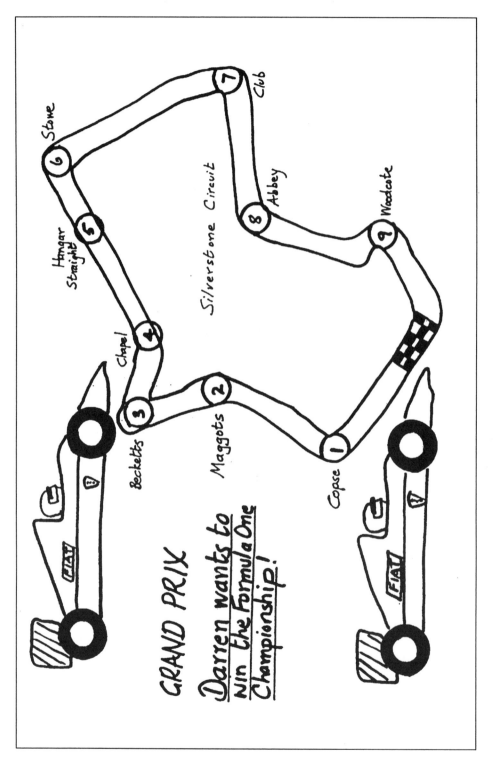

Figure 5.2 Example of a tailor-made self monitoring behaviour chart

Stage 4: Evaluate success
Repeat the observation exercise in Stage 2, and compare new data with base-line data. If you are satisfied that progress has been made, a similar kind of programme can be devised for more challenging tasks and different behaviours. If the data shows lack of progress, the programme may need to be re-run with tighter controls, e.g. longer on the earlier steps.

Stage 5: Phase out the tangible rewards
Once progress is evident, revert to praise, displaying work and other customary ways of reinforcing good behaviour and effort.

HYPERACTIVITY

There are some children who, both at home and in school, have chronic behaviour problems. They have difficulty in sustaining attention and controlling their movements; they act impulsively. When such symptoms begin before the age of seven, persist for at least six months, and are significantly impairing the child's school work, personal relationships and general functioning at home and school, the term Attention-Deficit Hyperactivity Disorder (ADHD) is sometimes applied. This was originally coined by the American Psychiatric Association, and is now gaining some currency in this country. According to one authority in the field, up to 7 per cent of children (more often boys than girls) may be so diagnosed (Hinshaw, 1994), though other estimates are lower.

Children with ADHD are said to have short attention spans, are easily distracted, and frequently don't carry out instructions or do as they are told. They have problems concentrating, engaging in tasks that require sustained mental effort and keeping track of their possessions. They have difficulty in playing or working quietly and in sitting still. They want to be 'on the go' much of the time. They appear clumsy, disorganised and forgetful. They find it hard to wait their turn in conversation or in group activities; in general they don't get on with their peers, yet deny that their behaviour is the cause of this.

This section can deal only very briefly with the problem of ADHD as it affects the classroom teacher. It will not attempt to explore the various theories about the causes of the disorder, to describe formal screening devices, or to suggest possible medication and diet. It should be stressed, however, that the disorder is not thought to have its origins in bad parenting, but is attributed to a range of interacting influences, including hereditary factors and neurological dysfunctioning. Although there appears to be no cure, teachers and parents can take steps to help the child manage more successfully. The points below have been made by authorities in the field, principally Goldstein and Goldstein (1992), Mould (1993) and Roth (1995). Note how many of these reflect aspects of effective teaching for all children.

- It is important to understand that the child is not deliberately being difficult and does have problems in understanding the effects of his behaviour. Constant nagging and punishment will be pointless and probably counter-productive. Try to avoid becoming frustrated and irritable but to see the world through the child's eyes.
- Work closely with the parents, facilitating regular and frequent exchanges on the child's progress. Encourage the parents to seek specialist help, and suggest reading specially written for parents (see Further Reading section).
- Because the hyperactive child has difficulty in working towards long-term goals, he needs a highly structured and predictable environment, such as that described in the previous section. Simple rules, rewards and sanctions should be consistently applied.
- Present work as a series of small, manageable steps with brief instructions, repeated as necessary and presented in different ways. Be willing to compromise and change tack in the light of experience.
- Go out of your way to find the positive and worthwhile characteristics of the child. Promise rewards for achieving specified targets. Give praise and rewards for appropriate work and behaviour as immediately as possible. Learn which particular measures are reinforcing for this particular child.
- The child will work better if seated at his own table, if possible with additional supervision, but allow movement within the room.
- Because the child is easily distracted, he needs prompts (but not hectoring) to keep him on-task when distracted. Try a friendly question ('John, how is your maths going?') or remind him of the reward ('John, what did we agree would happen when you finished that?'), and avoid blame-attributing remarks ('John, get on with your work!') or threats ('John, if you don't finish that you won't get that smiley sticker').
- To get on with others, the child needs help in defining problems and implementing solutions. Goldstein and Goldstein suggest working with the parents to find a social problem which the child recognises (e.g. constant disagreement with another child) even if this is not exactly how you see it. Then get the child to suggest a few solutions and then choose one. Help him to realise the steps needed to achieve success and to practice these with you before practising them with others. Discuss the results.
- Provide simple structures by which the child can become more socially competent. Goldstein and Goldstein suggest teaching steps which enable the child to develop skills in areas such as listening to others, meeting new people, starting and ending a conversation, giving self-award, following instructions, sharing, playing and working cooperatively, saying thank you, offering and accepting a compliment, understanding how his behaviour affects others and how others feel, and apologising.

- Remembering that the child lacks social competencies, give positive directions to change unwanted behaviour. Tell the child what you want rather than what you don't want. Any punishment, such as time-out, should be brief (just one minute is often appropriate) and executed firmly. Return the child to the problem situation and request compliance.

CHAPTER 6

Developing A Whole-School Behaviour Policy

> Head teachers and teachers should, in consultation with governors, develop and act upon whole-school behaviour policies which are clearly understood by pupils, parents and other school staff.
>
> *DfE Circular 8/94*, para. 18

The purpose of a whole-school behaviour policy is to promote consensus amongst members of the school community about expected standards of behaviour and how these might be realised and maintained. The justification for a collaborative approach to behaviour policy was discussed in Chapter 1(see pp.12–16). The purpose of this chapter is to look at some of the particular ways in which schools might go about the making and reviewing of their behaviour policy by involving not only all the teachers but also support staff, mid-day supervisors, governors, parents, and – most important – the pupils themselves.

Perhaps the best demonstration that whole-school policies 'work' comes from the experience of a DfE-funded project in which the majority of schools in Sheffield participated in a range of whole-school strategies to combat bullying (see pp.128–29). This project showed how time spent on the development of a behaviour policy paid off in improving relationships and in helping pupils to feel more able to discuss personal problems. There is also evidence that whole-school behaviour policies can reduce teacher stress arising from disruptive behaviour, whilst also changing staff behaviour through promoting a more widespread and consistent use of pro-active strategies to encourage pupils, such as praise, positive body language, and utilising pupils' ideas (Bain *et al.*, 1991).

There are five essential features in a whole-school behaviour policy:

1   *It is unique to the individual school.* Of course, there are many sorts of approaches that constitute 'good practice' everywhere. But no two schools have the same pupils, staff, parents or site, and therefore each will have concerns that are special to it. Whole-school policies cannot therefore be simply 'imported' from other schools or books such as this one. They have to be specially thought through, even though ideas may be borrowed from other sources.

2   *It should be pro-active rather than re-active.* The main emphasis should be on generating a set of general principles, identifying the behaviour problems in the school, and then agreeing a range of strategies that are consistent with the governing principles.

3   *It is **by** the whole school.* Everyone is involved – all the adults who work in the school (including support teachers and mid-day supervisors), pupils, parents, and governors.

4   *It is **for** the whole school.* The policy covers not only general conduct and pupil-adult relationships, but also behaviour between pupils. It is about respecting persons rather than deferring to status; it needs to address problems of discrimination. As Thompson and Sharp (1994, p.3) point out:

> Whether aiming to tackle racism, sexism, bullying or harassment and rejection of students with special educational needs, the core principle of any behaviour policy will be to challenge negative discrimination and to promote constructive relationship skills.

It can also involve relationships between staff, for instance, in the way decisions are reached in the school and who should know what.

5   *It is included in the School Development Plan* and is linked quite explicitly with other school policies. These will include areas of the curriculum that have an obvious part to play in the development of children's behaviour (such as English and Drama, RE, PSE) and other general curricular policies such as those on ethnicity, gender and special educational needs.

STAGES IN DEVELOPING OR REVIEWING A WHOLE-SCHOOL BEHAVIOUR POLICY

A frequent comment from those who have been involved in the development of a whole-school behaviour policy is that the *process* of policy-making itself materially affects relationships in school. However, such an experience is not inevitable. It depends upon the degree to which various conditions have been observed:

- Have the stages of planning been carefully defined?
- Has proper attention been given to raising awareness among all parts of the school community?
- Has the consultation been wide in its scope and carried out in a spirit of genuine partnership?
- Have difficult problems been thoroughly thought through?
- Does the process of drawing up the actual policy statement and supporting action plans properly reflect what has been agreed?

The evidence suggests that where the process is not properly thought out and its importance recognised (perhaps because staff thought it would be unduly time-consuming), the outcome is disappointing (Smith, 1994; Thompson and Sharp, 1994). There are no short cuts to developing a whole-school policy on behaviour.

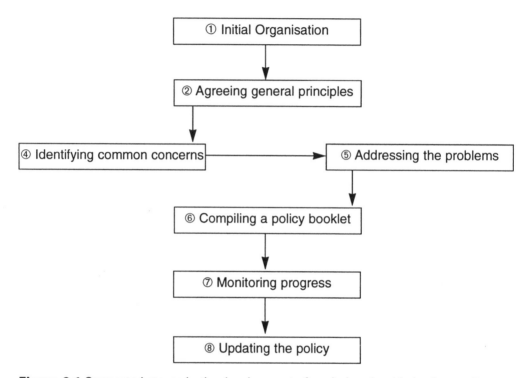

Figure 6.1 Suggested stages in the development of a whole-school behaviour policy

Figure 6.1 outlines the series of stages which a school might go through in the development or reviewing process. The first stage of *initial organisation* might include the following:

- Ensuring that policy development forms part of the school's development plan, with implications for the allocation of funds for in-service training.
- Appointing someone to coordinate the policy, and ensuring that they have the opportunity to attend relevant courses. Some schools believe that the 'someone' is best not the headteacher to avoid the danger of the policy being thought of as 'his' or 'hers' rather than 'ours'; however, the head should take a leading role if the project is to be given status. Some schools have also found it helpful to have an assistant coordinator from outside the staff, such as an interested governor or parent. Another approach is to set up a steering

group which includes one or two non-teacher representatives as well as teaching staff.

- Arranging a planning day to get the policy off the ground (or for a major review, if a previous policy needs updating). Here it is important to invite all the adults who work in the school plus governors. Parent representation is not a straightforward matter, but certainly the parent governors should be invited and representatives of the school's parent association. Parents in general can be invited to contribute suggestions, or the topic can be raised at the annual parents' meeting or at a special workshop for parents. An outside speaker is often helpful in stimulating interest, introducing new ideas and acting as an independent facilitator.

- Agreeing a timetable for developing the policy. Most schools have found that about a term and a half is needed. Much less, and there is insufficient time to think things through properly and involve the pupils; much longer, and motivation may be difficult to maintain. However, aspects of the policy can obviously be implemented as they are agreed.

- Giving the project a positive-sounding title, such as 'Improving Relationships'.

The next stage, that of establishing a set of *general principles* which will govern the whole behaviour policy, is sometimes overlooked in the rush to get new strategies off the ground, but it is important if the exercise is to be given coherence. Everyone must be clear what their endeavours are all about. One way of organising this stage is to arrange a joint meeting of staff and governors. At this point, comments and suggestions should be freely accepted without undue evaluation. The ideas can then used by a steering group to give shape to, say, half-a-dozen procedural principles which will govern all the more detailed approaches to be determined later. Examples are principles about caring, cooperating, respecting individuality and consideration for others.

The third stage, that of *identifying common concerns*, might suitably form an important part of a special planning day. The writer has found the following method to be generally successful in involving everyone and getting priorities straight with an economical use of time.

- The meeting divides into groups of six to eight, each including members from the various constituencies (teachers, support and ancillary staff, mid-day supervisors, governors, parents) as far as possible. Each group has a facilitator and a recorder.

- Each group is given one specific location in the school to focus on, such as classrooms, assembly, play areas, lunchroom, around the school, and perhaps also to and from school. In a large school, a location may be assigned to more than one group.

- The groups have, say, 15 minutes to engage members in two activities with regard to their assigned location: *brainstorming* to elicit all the main concerns of group members regarding behaviour in the location; and then *prioritising*, say, three of these and recording the behaviours with large letters on strips of card about 450cm by 100cm. It helps to use different colours for the different locations

- With everyone re-assembled and sitting in a horse-shoe, one facilitator presents the group's prioritised concerns. This is done by laying the cards on the floor in a column somewhat to the left of the centre of the space within the horseshoe and saying something briefly about each concern.

- A second facilitator does likewise, but, if there is any overlap with the concerns of the first group, the relevant card is placed to the right of the other group's card. The other facilitators follow suit.

- When all groups have completed their presentations, it should be clearly apparent from reading the cards on the floor what the main concerns are (each row), as shown in the example in Figure 6.2. Where group feelings overlap (adjacent cards), a label could be given to cover them all. These findings are then noted by the policy coordinator.

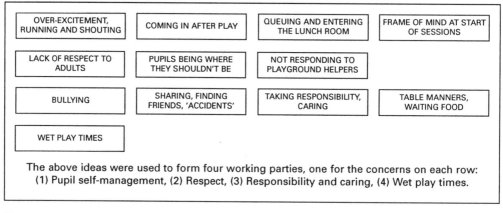

OVER-EXCITEMENT, RUNNING AND SHOUTING	COMING IN AFTER PLAY	QUEUING AND ENTERING THE LUNCH ROOM	FRAME OF MIND AT START OF SESSIONS
LACK OF RESPECT TO ADULTS	PUPILS BEING WHERE THEY SHOULDN'T BE	NOT RESPONDING TO PLAYGROUND HELPERS	
BULLYING	SHARING, FINDING FRIENDS, 'ACCIDENTS'	TAKING RESPONSIBILITY, CARING	TABLE MANNERS, WAITING FOOD
WET PLAY TIMES			

The above ideas were used to form four working parties, one for the concerns on each row:
(1) Pupil self-management, (2) Respect, (3) Responsibility and caring, (4) Wet play times.

Figure 6.2 One school's behavioural concerns as identified using the 'card system' at a behaviour policy planning day

The initial brainstorming in location groups gives everyone a chance to have a say, while the physical act of placing cards on the floor and attending to their configuration helps to focus everyone's attention on the expressed concerns of the groups and to share ideas.

The next stage, *addressing the problems*, can proceed as the next agenda item for the planning day, or it can be taken up at a later point (but not too much later lest the momentum is lost). Working groups on each of the identified concerns can be formed to discuss appropriate strategies. The groups are best made up of a cross-section of constituencies, as far as possible. Even if a concern is essentially confined to a specific location (e.g. how children enter the classroom and settle down for the session), it is useful to have adults with different sorts of responsibilities present because children's behaviour in one location is often a consequence of what has happened in a previous one. If the problem is, say, entering the classroom after the lunch break, the mid-day supervisors as well as teaching staff need to discuss it. Also, the opportunity is given for those with different roles in the school to learn from each other, so that the exercise itself contributes to a whole-school view.

It is important for each group to have regard for the four broad types of strategy outlined at the end of Chapter 1 (see pp.16–18). Indeed, it might be helpful if each group is given the framework suggested in Figure 6.3 to help ensure that the four main types of approach are considered.

Problem:	
① **What strategies could pre-empt the problem?**	② **How can we most effectively respond to incidents of the problem behaviour?**
③ **How can good behaviour be promoted?**	④ **How can good behaviour be reinforced?**

Figure 6.3 Framework for developing whole-school strategies with respect to an identified problem

As various policy statements are agreed, they can be assembled into a *behaviour policy booklet*. The contents of this will obviously vary according to the needs of the school, but the sorts of items in Checklist 6.1 could be considered. The governing body (which at the start helped to set out general principles for behaviour policy) might then be invited to comment on the booklet and in due course to endorse it. One advantage of assembling a range of behaviour policy statements into a single booklet is that the school then has an official record not only for general staff use but for new teachers, supply staff, new support and ancillary staff, new mid-day supervisors, student teachers and others who visit the school. This should help maintain a consistency of approach, which is one of the purposes of a whole-school policy.

Checklist 6.1
Possible items for inclusion in a booklet on school behaviour

✓ general principles and aims governing the behaviour policy
✓ links with other policies (e.g. on gender, special needs, race and those whose mother tongue is not English)
✓ specific target behaviours to be encouraged, particularly with regard to the concerns expressed at the general planning meeting
✓ agreed Codes of Conduct (e.g. general school rules; playground code)
✓ guidelines for staff in:
  • preventing unwanted behaviour
  • reinforcing good behaviour (e.g. praise and rewards; certificates for good behaviour; ways of informing parents of progress)
  • responding to unwanted behaviour (e.g. styles of reprimand; approved punishments; procedures for referral to senior staff, for involving parents and for referral for special support)
  • developing behaviour through curriculum work (e.g. role-play; literature; measures to raise self-esteem and feelings of competency; cooperative learning)
✓ guidelines for playground procedures (e.g. supervision styles; dealing with incidents; promoting good behaviour; facilities and equipment for wet playtimes)
✓ guidelines for dealing with incidents of bullying, including supporting victims and helping perpetrators to change their behaviour
✓ arrangements for involving in on-going behaviour policy (e.g. a school council; Quality Circles)
✓ guidelines for school absence – what parents and teachers are expected to do
✓ names of relevant people to give advice and support (e.g. the Coordinator of Behaviour Policy; any teacher who acts as a counsellor for bullied children)

The school's behaviour policy will need to be *monitored*. This is important not only in its own right, to see if all is going as planned, but also to keep up the momentum. Although whole-school policies can and do change staff and pupil behaviour, experience suggests there is a real danger of regression when the novelty begins to wear off and intervention strategies and monitoring are relaxed (Bain *et al.*, 1991).

The system of monitoring should be built in from the start so that each of the working groups will have suggested means by which the school can know if the policy is working. Thompson and Sharp (1994) suggest three types of data which can be collected for monitoring purposes:

1   *Changes in the behaviour and attitude of people in the school.* This could include special surveys to elicit pupils' opinions (e.g. on bullying – see pp.134–35) or focused observation and record-keeping over a limited period of time (e.g. for one week staff keep records of behaviour according to agreed criteria).

2   *Management data collected routinely.* Examples are the number of referrals to the senior staff for incidents of bullying, on the number of occasions parents have complained about behaviour or have been asked to come to the school to discuss their child's conduct. The means by which such records are kept may need to be examined.

3   *Utilisation of the procedures in the policy.* Examples could include the use of a playground behaviour book (see next chapter, pp.120–21), or the experience of staff who have used circle times (see pp.61–2) and Quality Circles (see pp.136–8), or the effectiveness of a newly-instituted School Council (see pp.110–13).

Once a year there needs to be a formal *policy review*. This may seem a bit extravagant on time when staff are concerned with so much policy development these days. The reason for holding a review so frequently is two-fold. First, there is little point in monitoring the agreed approaches and strategies if there is no facility for changing the policy in the light of the findings. Secondly, behaviour policy statements must continuously reflect the needs of the changing school population. Every year children leave and new children (and new parents) arrive; those who stay probably have new class teachers. There may be new members of the teaching and support staff who need to be consulted so that the concept of ownership remains a key characteristic of the behaviour policy statements. And, of course, the pupils need fresh opportunities each year to engage in discussion about such matters as their school rules and the playground code so that these too remain 'owned'.

INVOLVING PUPILS IN POLICY DEVELOPMENT

In the previous section, the stages listed in Figure 6.2 were discussed mainly in relation to the perceptions of adults in the school. But, as argued earlier, it is crucial that the pupils should be actively involved too. Two notes of caution are needed here, however.

First of all, there is always a danger that pupils' participation in policy-making will amount to tokenism rather than genuine empowerment. Tokenism can arise if pupils are asked to contribute suggestions but their ideas are not properly discussed or they are left unsure of the extent to which their contributions have been taken seriously. The school staff will need to decide at what level to involve pupils, that is whether just to consult them about behaviour policy or to involve them as partners. If the concept of partnership is accepted, then pupils need a power base for sharing responsibility in some significant area of decision-making, particularly in matters which materially affect their relationships with each other, such as playground life and bullying.

Secondly, it is obviously unreasonable to expect pupils to act as partners in policy-making if they are inexperienced in cooperative learning situations. The assumption made in this chapter is that the children are used to working collaboratively in pairs and small groups (Chapter 4, pp.68–73) and that their involvement in behaviour policy is effectively an extension of this ethos of cooperation rather than an innovation. Note that empowering pupils to contribute to the school's behaviour policy is not something extra which is completed outside the main curriculum but is integral to it. Not only are there many suitable activities which can be carried out during normal lesson time, but even those taking place during lunchtimes or after school (e.g. meetings of a School Council) can properly be regarded as part of the curriculum since they play a central part in the children's social and emotional development.

Many of the specific ways of engaging pupils in this sort of exercise are outlined in other chapters, as shown in Checklist 6.2. In the remainder of this chapter we look at two other strategies – developing a school code and instituting a School Council.

Checklist 6.2
Some ways of involving children in the development of a behavioural policy

	See Chapter:
✓ Classroom rules	2
✓ Reward system/privilege time	3 & 5
✓ Circle-time	4
✓ Individual behaviour plans	5
✓ School behaviour code	6
✓ School Council	6
✓ Identifying playground problems	7
✓ Playground code	7
✓ Development of school environment	7
✓ Data on bullying	8
✓ Quality Circles	8
✓ Responding to bullying incidents	8

Developing a school code

It may sound like a thoroughly impracticable proposition to involve all the

Term 1

Generating the code

SERIES OF ASSEMBLIES
(1) Discussion on the theme 'taking pride in our school'
(2) Gathering ideas for a school code based on this theme
(3) Unpacking each item in the agreed code

CLASSWORK
(1) Further discussion on the code
(2) Making illustrations for a display about the code
(3) Making miniatures of the illustrations for a school book on the code

CORRIDOR
Mounting a display to communicate the rules

Term 2

Communicating and Reinforcing the code

ASSEMBLY AND CLASSROOM
Reinforcing the code through reminders and posters in each classroom

PARENTS
Communicating the code to parents to widen the scope for enforcement of the code

Term 3 and subsequently

Reinforcing the code

ASSEMBLY AND CLASSROOM
Frequent referral to the code

Figure 6.4 How Woodville School involved the children in developing a school code of conduct

children in generating a school code of behaviour. But if pupils have already had experience in formulating rules for their classroom (see pp.20–25), it should not be too difficult to devise a means whereby they can be actively engaged in rule-making for the school as a whole. Many primary schools have decided that the process is both worthwhile and interesting, as illustrated in the following example from Woodville Junior School in Surrey.

The staff of this school agreed that their commitment to 'working in partnership' meant that all members of the team had an opinion that was valuable to everyone, and that the team included the children as well as the adults in the school. They therefore decided to involve all the children in formulating a school code of conduct. At the same time, they appreciated that to engage the pupils' interest effectively required a clear, agreed framework. A structured sequence of events, to take place over two terms and involving all the pupils and teaching staff, was planned and implemented. These events, summarised in Figure 6.4, will now be briefly explained.

The process began with a school assembly in which the head teacher stimulated a discussion centred around the question 'What does it mean to be proud of something?'. The idea of 'taking pride in our school' soon developed, and the assembly decided that a set of statements should be drawn up to establish expectations for all pupils and so make the school even more deserving of everyone's pride. In the next assembly, ideas for these statements were gathered from the pupils and a list of 25 items was recorded, using an overhead projector. Overlaps between the items were noted, and the statements were then grouped around certain themes, such as 'working hard' and 'caring'. Following this assembly, a staff team worked together to tidy up the statements. They reduced the number to nine and began each item with 'We ...' to emphasise the community ethos. The proposed list was then presented to the children in a third assembly, and comments were invited. Although the staff were willing to negotiate on the items, no one expressed disagreement and the pupils then voted unanimously for the code to be adopted. The statements were:

In Woodville ...
- We work hard and always try to do our best
- We are always polite, helpful and honest
- We care for everyone
- We know when it is time to listen quietly
- We always try to keep ourselves and others safe
- We always try to look smart
- We keep our school neat and tidy
- We look after our own and other people's property
- We work as a team and value other people

We are proud of Woodville School.

For the remainder of the term assemblies on Mondays were devoted to developing the code. Each member of staff took one of the nine statements and unpacked it with the children and collected their ideas about the range of matters that the statement encompassed. All the teachers made a point of attending these assemblies so that everyone knew what was being decided. The staff had previously discussed points which they would want to ensure were included in the discussion, particularly those to do with safety; but most of the initiative came from the children. For example, during the assembly when the statement about being polite, helpful and honest was discussed, the children came up with these ideas (put into sentences by the teacher):

We always say 'Please' and 'Thank you'.
We always say sorry if we have upset someone, adult or child, or done something wrong.
We always hold the door open if there is someone coming through behind us.
We never take things which do not belong to us.
We always offer to help if we can.
We are always kind to everyone in the school, even if they are not a friend
We never swear.

Similarly, the assembly whose responsibility was to unpack the statement about keeping the school neat and tidy came up with suggestions such as 'We always put litter in the bin even if it isn't our litter' and 'We always put equipment back where it belongs', and so on. The sub-statements on looking smart gave details of the school uniform.

The last assembly of the term was used to bring everything together, reflecting on what had been achieved and generally raising awareness about the implications of the statements and sub-statements which comprised the new school code.

During the following term the code was reinforced through work in lesson time. The children in each class took one of the statements in the code, discussed it further and made paintings to illustrate ways in which the meanings of the sub-statements could be expressed in practice. A display was then mounted. Each main statement was placed in large letters in the middle and the illustrations for the sub-statements were arranged around it with suitable captions. The displays from all the classes were posted along a corridor near the school entrance and given the general title 'We are proud to be part of Woodville School'. The children were encouraged to look at everyone's efforts and to engage the interest of school visitors in the project. In a further activity that term, the children made miniature versions of their pictures; these were compiled into a book which is kept in the library and frequently referred to. The code was also sent to all parents, who were invited to support the school in ensuring that it was observed. Additionally, a poster displaying the statements was placed in each classroom to remind pupils what had been agreed. An empty box was added in which class teachers could draw attention to any item which some children were failing to acknowledge in their behaviour. In subsequent assemblies and lessons during the year, regular reminders were issued to emphasise the importance of observing the code.

The school staff is convinced that this exercise was a valuable experience for everyone and that standards of behaviour improved as a result. When the writer visited the school, a group of children, with great pride, explained the corridor display and the library book of miniatures, recounting the events that had stimulated its production. Certainly no visitor to the school could fail to be impressed by the way the children conduct themselves.

The success of partnership enterprises such as the one just described clearly depends on the staff's willingness to surrender the traditional authority structure based on 'upward respect' in favour of one grounded in the principle of mutual respect. But it is also conditional upon the staff providing a clear sense of direction and a structure which supports pupil empowerment. A good deal of work is involved and the process takes time, but the activities are fun and the children, from all accounts, enjoy it and respond positively to its objectives.

School councils

Elected school councils offer a permanent structure by which pupils are continuously involved in decision-making and are encouraged to assume greater levels of responsibility than might otherwise be the case. Although in the past they have been mainly a feature of some secondary and 'progressive' schools, they are now becoming more popular in primary schools. As the Speaker's Commission on Citizenship (Stonecroft, 1990) observed:

> Democracy is best learned in a democratic setting where participation is encouraged, where views can be expressed openly and discussed, where there is freedom of expression for pupils and teachers, and where there is fairness and justice.

The way councils work in primary schools typically follows the patterns noted by Brading (1989) in his evaluation of the innovation in four London primary schools. The main features are summarised in Figure 6.5. A council typically comprises one boy and one girl from each class in Years 3 to 6 and meets four or five times a term. The councillors are elected by their classes for at least one term and one of them agrees to act as minute secretary. Although council meetings are usually chaired by the headteacher or another member of staff, class meetings which take place between council meetings are typically chaired by one of the class councillors. These latter meetings are extremely important, for they enable all pupils to play a meaningful part in the council

School Council

✔ **2 reps from each class**

✔ **head or teacher chairs**

✔ **child takes minutes**

✔ **meets, say, monthly**

✔ **class meetings between to report back and set agenda**

✖ **no person to be named in critical comments**

✔ **rota of classes to observe**

✔ **typical matters discussed:**
- **name-calling**
- **wet lunchtimes**
- **playground equipment**
- **lining-up procedures**
- **raising money for charities**

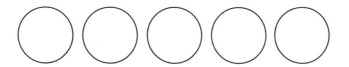

Figure 6.5

proceedings. Their purpose is to receive reports from the previous council meeting and then to gather suggestions for the agenda of the next council meeting. Some pupil councils issue regular newsletters or have their own notice board or slot in assembly.

Certain constraints are usually imposed upon a council's powers: for instance, the head's intervention would normally be required for important changes of policy, and there are usually rules of procedure to help the children conduct meetings in a constructive way. For instance, councillors are not customarily allowed to make negative remarks about named individuals. None the less, the matters debated are real issues which materially affect the children's lives and relate to their personal problems. Examples of items included in typical agendas are:

- name-calling and other aspects of bullying
- lining up procedures
- playground facilities and games
- activities for wet playtimes
- school uniform
- lunch menus
- raising money for school equipment or for charities
- sanctions and rewards
- clubs and other extra-curricular activities.

Although the problems are likely to be much the same from one school to another, each council will produce its unique solution. In one school, Brading found that the council dealt with the problem of ball games dominating tarmac space by agreeing to designate certain areas of the playground for this purpose, while in another school nearby the council dealt with the same problem by declaring Wednesday a 'no football' day.

A matter that needs discussion in all-through primary schools concerns the position of the infants in relation to the school council. Children below the age of seven or eight are usually considered too young and inexperienced to play a direct part in council meetings. At the same time, it would be a pity to exclude their involvement altogether. A further issue is the danger of the council becoming an élitist group, whose workings remain rather mysterious to the rest of the school in spite of the intervening class meetings. Ways of getting round both these problems were instituted in Brading's own school. Key Stage 1 children were represented by top junior children, who visited the infant classrooms to gather suggestions and report back to council meetings. The school organised a rota whereby each class and its teacher took turns to observe council meetings, thus enabling all children to understand the way councils conduct their business and deal with problems when disagreements arise.

Whilst councils are generally very successful in engaging pupil involvement and preparing for citizenship, they are not without their problems. Some schools have faced difficulties in running council meetings fairly or have found that some decisions have proved unpopular or unworkable. However, such experiences are best regarded as part of the children's social education and training in democratic procedures. A degree of risk is entailed in deciding to set up a school council, but the likelihood of the council becoming discredited and floundering is small provided the staff are prepared to support pupils when problems arise. In the writer's experience, most councils in primary schools are effective and the pupils take their responsibilities seriously. From responses to a questionnaire in his sample schools, Brading found that pupils value the opportunity to express their feelings and bring about change. As one child simply but reassuringly put it: 'I think it's a good idea to have a school council because it makes the school a happier place to be in'.

Involving children in the development of a behaviour policy is not easy, but it can be tremendously rewarding and effective. At the heart of the process must be a preparedness by the staff and governing body to enter into a spirit of partnership with the children. This certainly does not mean that teachers are simple facilitators: there is a vital role of leadership to play. But it is a not a leadership which tells children just what to do and not to do – or, as our political masters sometimes simplistically put it, 'to teach them the difference between right and wrong'. Rather it is a leadership which is embedded in the context of educating the emotions, refining beliefs and promoting personal skills. It stimulates children to make a stand against indifference and inaction. It raises awareness about the way in which individuals and groups suffer from discrimination, rejection or being disregarded. It emphasises the inter-dependence of each member of the school community and how the behaviour of any one party affects, and is affected by, others. It sets up a framework for structured discussion, promotes a deeper and more mutual understanding of the issues and personal dilemmas which affect the children's everyday lives and teaches children the skills involved in communicating and exchanging ideas. Crucially, it sets high expectations and makes demands on children by valuing their perspective and capacity to offer constructive ideas and suggestions.

CHAPTER 7

Playtime and Lunchtime

> We were told at several schools that the supervision of pupils at lunchtime is the biggest single behaviour-related problem that they face.
>
> *Elton Report*, para.4.135

The importance of developing a playground and lunchtime policy cannot be over-emphasised. Consider the following findings from recent research studies:

- Seven–year–olds spend about a quarter of their school time in the playground or lunchroom – as much time as they spend on the 3Rs (Tizard *et al.*, 1988)
- Most playground behaviour is friendly and sociable, but teasing, name-calling, fighting, being·out in the cold, having nothing to do, or not having equal opportunities to engage in play are concerns for a significant minority, especially girls (Blatchford *et al.*, 1990; Mooney *et al.*, 1991)
- Most bullying takes place in the playground (Smith and Sharp, 1994)
- Few school playgrounds or play areas meet the needs children express (Lucas, 1994)
- 11-year-olds have strong views about life in the playground and also many sensible ideas about how it could be improved (Blatchford *et al.*, 1990)
- There is clear evidence that schools can do a great deal to improve playground behaviour and reduce bullying (Boulton, 1994a)
- Well-planned intervention strategies and regular monitoring appreciably reduce all forms of bullying in the playground (Whitney *et al.*, 1994).

There is no doubt that playtime is popular with most children and is an important part in the learning of social skills. There is also clear evidence that the longer children are confined indoors, the more vigorous their activity in subsequent outdoor play (Pellegrini and Davis, 1993). None the less, many pupils experience problems such as racism, sexism, bullying and aggression. Fortunately, we know from the evidence of recent studies that much can be done to combat these behaviours, but only if there is a concerted whole-school policy involving not only all the adults in the school – including, most importantly, the midday supervisors – but the pupils as well. As Blatchford and Sharp (1994) point out, the views of the children and supervisors must be taken on board if a playground policy is to be effective: they have special, even unique, knowledge of what goes on in the playground.

IDENTIFYING NEEDS AND PROBLEMS

The main aspects of playground policy development are shown in Figure 7.1. The first objective is ascertaining the problems and needs. For this, a consultation exercise needs to be organised to elicit information from pupils, teachers, supervisors and parents.

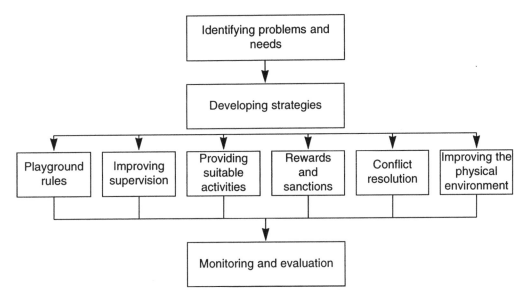

Figure 7.1 Developing playground and lunchtime policy

The pupils' perspective

There are many ways of involving the pupils in identifying playground and lunchtime problems, ranging from discussion in class and assembly to more sophisticated devices such as Quality Circles, as outlined in Chapter 8, or a School Council, as explained in Chapter 6. Whatever the forum for discussion, it is often more productive if data on pupils' experiences and views have first been collected in a systematic way, such as by means of a questionnaire. As Ross and Ryan (1994) describe in their case study, a questionnaire can help to establish the various ways pupils spend their time in the playground, their likes and dislikes about playtime and the prevalence of various problems and their causes. In another case study, Pat White (1988) gives an account of the way the playground experiences of children were discovered through an analysis of their writings and drawings. Two representatives from each class compiled

116

summaries of the children's perceptions which were used for subsequent discussion. The material revealed many sad instances of 'preventable misery and distress,...petty spitefulness and unpleasantness' (p.195), which suggested that any effort to ameliorate such suffering would be worthwhile.

A range of other techniques has been developed by the Department of Landscape at Sheffield University (Sheat and Beer, 1994). A particularly successful strategy is to provide children with a large map of the school grounds, containing basic information such as buildings and boundaries. Without any prompting, the children are asked to record everything they can think of regarding what spaces there are, what goes on there, which spaces are most and least used, and what conflicts arise there. While the children are doing this, much interesting discussion ensues, and the results provide a great deal of information about the playground from the pupils' viewpoint. Another valuable strategy used by the Sheffield Landscape Department is a site walkabout exercise, in which small groups of pupils take visitors round the grounds and are invited, in strict confidence, to 'spill the beans' – which in practice they readily do! A third technique is to give small groups of children disposable cameras to take five shots which best represent the way they view the school. The children then make a display of the pictures with supporting statements and comments.

For more ideas, the reader is referred to Ross and Ryan's excellent book *Can I Stay In Today Miss?* (1990). This includes items for a playground questionnaire, structures for conducting interviews and instructions for carrying out investigative mapwork. It also describes how to use 'trigger cards', containing statements about the positive and negative aspects of playground life; pupils rank each of these according to a specified criterion (e.g. 'What happens most often?) and share their evaluations.

The teachers' and supervisors' perspective

The concerns of the teaching staff and supervisors can be identified and shared through joint meetings, using the system of 'brainstorming' and prioritising suggested in the previous chapter (pp. 101–102). Other possibilities are to invite supervisors to give a presentation to a staff meeting (Sharp, 1994) or to interview supervisors individually. Using this latter method, one school, described by Ross and Ryan (1994) not only learned about the supervisors' concerns relating to safety, the dominance of space by football games, and children being excluded from groups, but also about their crying need for clear rules and back-up from the staff. The exercise also indicated the supervisors' feelings of low status in the school community, which they found puzzling in view of their potential to help the staff through liaising with parents who lived near them.

Parents' perspective

It is also important to find out the perceptions of parents to ensure that a comprehensive picture of playground life emerges. In the White study referred to above, parents were invited to a special meeting to watch some children enact episodes of playground conflict; they then discussed the issues raised. In the Ross and Ryan study, parents participated through interviews about the issues raised by the children and supervisors. By adopting this procedure, the school was able to learn of the dilemmas faced by parents worrying about such problems as their child not wanting to go to school, girls being left out, racism and safety.

DEVELOPING A PLAYGROUND CODE

Fundamental to any playground policy is a code of behaviour. This helps to set the behaviour expectations which the school has for children, enables the supervisors to approach their responsibilities in a consistent manner and provides criteria for giving rewards and imposing sanctions. As with classroom and general school rules, a playground code is best limited to a few items which are positively expressed. Most importantly, as with identifying problems and needs, the process of determining the playground code should include the children's active participation.

A framework needs to be agreed for involving pupils in a constructive way. A model based on the experience of a number of schools is given in Figure 7.2. It assumes that the pupils have been engaged in consultation exercises such as those described in the previous section. During a series of exercises during assembly and class time, the children (with their teachers) use their findings about playground problems and needs to formulate a short set of playground rules. In the final stage, the parents are involved in a dialogue at home about what is acceptable playground behaviour and in helping to reinforce the code

In the White study the code which finally emerged after the pupils' suggestions had been discussed by staff read as follows:

1. We will always be kind and considerate to everybody in the playground.

2. We will look after the playground and make sure that it is always a nice place to be in.

3. We will share the playground space so that other games, besides football, can be played.

4. Even if we are in the midst of something very exciting or important, we will stop and listen to any instruction an adult may give us.

Rule 3 is interesting in the demands it makes on children to exercise

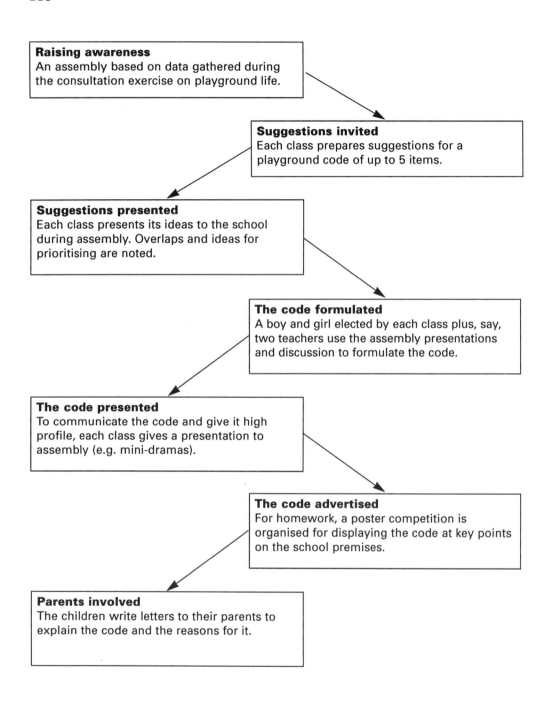

Raising awareness
An assembly based on data gathered during the consultation exercise on playground life.

Suggestions invited
Each class prepares suggestions for a playground code of up to 5 items.

Suggestions presented
Each class presents its ideas to the school during assembly. Overlaps and ideas for prioritising are noted.

The code formulated
A boy and girl elected by each class plus, say, two teachers use the assembly presentations and discussion to formulate the code.

The code presented
To communicate the code and give it high profile, each class gives a presentation to assembly (e.g. mini-dramas).

The code advertised
For homework, a poster competition is organised for displaying the code at key points on the school premises.

Parents involved
The children write letters to their parents to explain the code and the reasons for it.

Figure 7.2 Developing a playground code of behaviour

responsibility. An earlier regulation had limited football to certain times of the week, but it was later decided to give children the opportunity to share space themselves without this structure. Items similar to these are likely to emerge in any school, but it is the process of generating the code which is so important in giving the children ownership of the rules.

PLAYGROUND SUPERVISION

Inadequate playground supervision may be one reason why most bullying takes place during recess periods (Boulton, 1994b). Under the School Teachers' Pay and Conditions regulations, the head teacher is responsible for midday supervision, but teaching staff in maintained schools are not contractually obliged to carry out supervisory duties during the lunchtime break. The children are therefore usually supervised by parents and others specially employed for that purpose. While this assists the teaching staff in preserving their lunch period for relaxation (or, more realistically perhaps, preparation and meetings), supervisors often say that they are not always given the help they need to carry out their job effectively (Fell, 1994; Sharp, 1994). Their difficulties can be summarised in terms of five 'lacks' – lack of status, lack of role clarity, lack of training, lack of communication and lack of information.

Lack of status

Supervisors often complain that the children do not show them the same respect as they do the teaching staff, ignoring their instructions, not addressing them properly and in some cases being abusive. Staff and parents can even reinforce this perception in the way they respond to incidents when supervisors complain: e.g. contradicting the supervisors' instructions or not involving them in remedial action. The status of supervisors is also undermined if they are not given the same power as teaching staff to impose sanctions.

Clearly it is critical not only that supervisors are invited to discuss their roles and status with teaching staff, but that the pupils and parents are fully aware of the supervisors' responsibilities and authority. The Head might introduce supervisors in assembly, using this occasion to clarify the supervisors' authority-status, including such matters as how they should be addressed and their right to issue instructions and impose sanctions. If supervisors wear name tags, the children can more easily address them by name. If playground and lunchroom behaviour are made the topic for assembly at regular intervals, supervisors can at the very least be invited to attend and, better still, to participate as well.

Some schools, however, have gone further than this, linking each supervisor to a class in which she can spend a little time after lunch to discuss playground issues and also join in some class activities such as hearing children read. In this way, the supervisors learn the children's names and get to know them better in a less supervisory capacity. Also, as Boulton (1994c) points out, children who identify the lunchtime supervisor as one who has status in the school and whose views they value may be less likely to engage in bullying, while victims of bullying may be encouraged to confide in a supervisor whom they see as a friend.

One way of meeting the problem of discipline and sanctions, is to arm supervisors with a clear set of procedures. In a project set up by Imich and Jefferies (1989) in one large Essex primary school, a support teacher made observations in the dining hall for a period of three weeks, and the findings formed the basis of a series of meetings with teaching staff and helpers. From the discussion, a set of procedures was agreed and a written record made for the benefit of newly appointed helpers. Items included: admitting to the dining area only children who are behaving satisfactorily; not allowing children to leave until everyone at their table has finished and returned dishes and utensils; commending pupils and giving team points for good behaviour; informing class teachers about good behaviour so that the pupils concerned received further praise in the classroom. Not relying on tale-telling but reprimanding only when the misbehaviour has been observed or facts have been established.

A hierarchy of sanctions was also drawn up so that misbehaviour could be managed in a consistent way. For fairly minor offences, such as pushing, shouting or talking back, offenders had to sit on a chair facing a wall for five minutes in an area away from other children and under an assistant's supervision. For more serious misbehaviour, such as swearing or insolence, the helper issued the offender with a yellow card on which was recorded the helper's name, the date and the offence. The child had to obtain the helper's signature for good behaviour each day for a week and then see the headteacher for signing off. Three yellow cards resulted in a red card; parents were contacted and the child was suspended from school during lunchtime for a week. During assembly these arrangements were carefully explained to the children, who could ask questions and make further suggestions. The system led to improved behaviour between pupils and better relationships between pupils and helpers, who felt they were now better respected.

An alternative approach, and one preferred by the writer, is for teaching and supervisory staff to operate a system whereby offenders can be deprived of privileges. If the school has a weekly 'privilege time' (see p.49), as recommended by Jenny Mosley (1994), midday supervisors as well as teachers can make use of this time in the following way:

- issue a warning to the offender
- record the nature of the unwanted behaviour in a booklet
- pass on the particulars to the class teacher
- the teacher deprives the child of five minutes during 'privilege time'.

On a more positive note, those children whose behaviour has not prompted the supervisors to issue notes to teachers for a full term can then be presented with a lunchtime certificate by the supervisor. As Jenny Mosley comments, 'Children feel much safer once they are in a system that is consistently applied and upheld by all the adults, regardless of their roles' (p.10). More ideas for incentives which supervisors can offer are given in Mosley's excellent book *Turn Your School Around* (1994). These include stickers to commend particular sorts of good behaviour, responsibility badges for children who agree to help supervisors with specified tasks, and a record of the names of children whom supervisors wish to commend for a certificate of good behaviour.

Lack of role clarity and training

It is tough being a playground supervisor if no one has made clear just what your authority is. Examples of problems which can arise include: not being sure who should be in charge if a teacher is present in the area; teachers contradicting orders given by a supervisor; confusion over who is allowed to stay inside at lunchtime; whether the supervisor is also in charge of children who are indoors; what sanctions, if any, are available to the supervisor; and supervisors being given unmanageable or unrealistic tasks (Sharp, 1994). At the same time, the supervisor is often expected to attend to all manner of things: matters of safety, often exacerbated by the design of the playground and hidden corners; incidents of fighting, name-calling and other aspects of bullying; children who do not want to be outside, feel insecure, get upset and need comforting; children not complying with instructions and being rude; special instructions from the head or a teacher; recording for rewards or sanctions; general uncertainty about doing the right thing; encouraging constructive forms of play. All this when the ratio of children to supervisors could be more than 50 to 1 (Andrews and Hinton, 1991).

Fortunately, the training needs of supervisors are becoming more recognised, and some local authorities and individual schools now provide special courses. Drawing on the recent work of Boulton and Sharp (Boulton, 1994a, b, c; Sharp, 1994), Fell (1994), Imich and Jefferies (1989), and Mosely (1994), provision for training in the areas listed in Checklist 7.2 is likely to be productive. Some of these issues need special training courses, but most can be addressed at school level. At the very least, schools should make available to supervisors books and packs which are written for them, such as the OPTIS guide (OPTIS, 1986), or the 'Guidelines for lunchtime supervisors' in Mosley (1994).

Checklist 7.1
Training for Midday Supervisors

Does your school:
✓ help supervisors to feel valued members of staff, with an important role in the life of the school?
✓ clarify the supervisors' roles and responsibility, what sanctions are available, and channels for communication?
✓ encourage supervisors to share playground problems with the staff and to evaluate their seriousness?
✓ provide basic first-aid training?
✓ help supervisors to clarify concepts of bullying (e.g. whether teasing is bullying) and to examine their attitude towards bullying incidents?
✓ increase supervisors' observation skills (e.g. learning to distinguish between aggressive fighting/bullying and playful, rough-and-tumble activity)?
✓ support supervisors in their efforts to help children manage their play activities effectively and smoothly (e.g. in sharing playground equipment and the contents of activity boxes through managing a rota)?
✓ suggest ways of taking preventative action to minimise behaviour problems (e.g. keeping a careful watch on vulnerable children; being especially vigilant in areas where bullying tends to take place; having a set of procedures for entering and leaving the lunchroom?)
✓ encourage good behaviour through 'catching the child being good', using praise and a system of rewards?
✓ help supervisors to manage playground incidents calmly and fairly?
✓ help supervisors to be authoritative without being authoritarian – imposing sanctions in a consistent manner (e.g. through using a yellow and red card system or a privileges system – see text), without resorting to sarcasm, labelling, empty threats or regular referrals to teachers?
✓ share with supervisors the school's policy on such matters as racism, equal opportunities for boys and girls, and special education needs (and inviting supervisors to training days on these kinds of issues)?

On the question of training supervisors to distinguish between aggressive versus rough-and-tumble play, Boulton (1994c) suggests that the latter is more likely to be characterised by the following:

- smiling or laughing
- staying together afterwards
- allowing the other child to gain advantage for a period
- role-reversals
- restrained touches or blows
- usually only two children involved with few if any onlookers attracted.

Lack of communication and information

Clear channels of communication are essential for effective supervision since this will enable the teaching and playground staff to work together and adopt consistent responses to playground problems and ways of improving playground behaviour. Some schools find it helpful to appoint a senior supervisor who not only has a general overseer's role but also can facilitate communication with the head teacher. It is important, however, for communication to be two-way: not just the head and teaching staff telling the supervisors about this and that, but drawing on the supervisors' unique experience and knowledge. Any school which has involved supervisors in meetings with the teaching staff will know that they are invaluable in providing a diagnosis of the problems from their perspective and in providing useful suggestions on managing lunchtime issues.

If the supervisors are to be properly involved in the development of playground policy, they need be given an on-going structure for expressing concerns and making suggestions for their amelioration. Paying supervisors to attend teaching staff meetings on a regular basis is one way of addressing this issue; and where a schools council is in place (see pp.110–13), supervisors can have representation on that forum.

As far as information is concerned, supervisors obviously need to know the playground rules, fire-drill procedures, and what to do with children who don't feel well. But, more specifically, they also need to be entrusted with confidential information about children who have medical problems, whose behaviour is a cause for concern, or who are vulnerable to the behaviour of other children or otherwise insecure and unhappy (Sharp, 1994). Equally, teachers need to know from supervisors what incidents have occurred (both good and bad) and who has been involved.

PLAYGROUND ACTIVITIES

Among playground problems, one of the most important is that of children being bored and having nothing constructive to do. Aggressive behaviour and bullying are much more likely to occur in such circumstances (Blatchford, 1989). Many primary schools therefore ensure that children have access to equipment such as soft balls, hoops, bean bags, skipping ropes, big toys for the reception class, clothes to dress up in – as well as boxes of indoor games in each class for wet weather, plus, perhaps, the possibility of watching a video or having access to computer games. Some schools also arrange lunchtime clubs, such as art, computing, drama, chess and model-making.

There is also the problem of some children effectively hijacking large areas of play space for football and chasing games. There need to be rules to address this issue, perhaps allocating a limited period of time for such pursuits or, if there is room, demarcating a specific area. Equally, the needs of children who do not want to play games should be respected. Many schools now have quiet areas, with seats or 'pub benches' or mats and, ideally, tubs of plants and trellis work to screen off the area and give it a special relaxing ambience.

A further development involves encouraging children to play new games. Sometimes older members of the community are invited to teach games that have been forgotten. But many teachers also like to promote games that develop children's co-operative skills and help to improve relationships (for some suggestions, see the Further Reading section). A question which arises is whether supervisors should be encouraged to initiate and participate in playground games. On the face of it, this sounds like a good idea, but it may not be so simple. Boulton (1994b) has reviewed the case for and against encouraging supervisors to join in children's games. On the one hand, he notes that adult involvement can help to pre-empt problems associated with playground conflict and unpleasantness, offering children something positive to do and encouraging individuals of different ages, temperaments and backgrounds to mix with each other. On the other hand, children derive benefits from playing without the help of adults. They have the opportunity to develop skills in organising play activities, particularly those involving many children, and developing the social skills necessary to deal with situations of conflict. Perhaps, as Boulton suggests, a compromise position is sensible – introducing playground activities and friendly games but withdrawing after a short period.

CONFLICT RESOLUTION

Conflict is not necessarily something bad and to be avoided. As Sharp, Cooper and Cowie (1994) point out, apart from being an inevitable part of human existence, the experience can be a positive one, resulting in problems getting sorted out and better relationships established. What matters is how people respond to conflict. The role of the school is therefore not to frown on conflicts and regard them as an aspect of misbehaving; rather it is to teach children the skills in resolving them effectively. For this it is necessary to 'bring the playground into the classroom'.

Timothy Duax, an American teacher working in London, has demonstrated that children can gradually learn to become less aggressive towards each other if they are encouraged to reflect upon their emotions and reactions to situations in which they would ordinarily hit out physically or verbally (Duax, 1988). Through weekly class discussions and role play, he helped children to understand that we all have a need to gain attention and to assert ourselves, but that some people are better than others in satisfying this need without resorting to physical violence and verbal conflict. What he did was to present everyday situations to the class and ask, 'What would you do?', thus encouraging children to explore alternative responses to situations in which they might be tempted to get their own way through provoking conflict. Examples included how to share limited resources in the playground and how to respond to teasing or hitting. Not surprisingly, the children did not change their response patterns immediately, but they gradually learned to do so as they built up a repertoire of courses of action and were encouraged by their teacher to try these out as opportunities arose.

These teaching ideas can be further structured through getting children to engage in the 'win-win' negotiating process, as described by Sharp, Cooper and Cowie (1994). Using real or imaginary conflict situations, children in pairs (or small groups) go through the following steps:

- Think about what you want, and why you want it.
- Explain these carefully and precisely to your partners and listen to what they say about their needs and wants.
- Think of all the possible ways in which the problem might be solved, writing them down but not at this stage evaluating them ('brainstorming').
- Read through the ideas and choose one that will make everyone feel a winner (hence the term 'win-win').
- Agree on one idea and put this into a precise action plan.

Another approach to conflict resolution is through the strategy known as Quality Circles, described in the next chapter.

IMPROVING THE PHYSICAL ENVIRONMENT

Attention to playground design and strategies for improving the physical environment of the school grounds has received a boost in recent years from the work of Learning Through Landscapes and the Worldwide Fund for Nature (Lucas, 1994; Titman, 1993), and the Department of Landscape at Sheffield University (Sheat and Beer, 1994; Higgins, 1994a, b), What is particularly interesting about these studies is the way they extend the school's opportunities for involving pupils and giving them a sense of ownership of playground developments.

Schools that have the cash, or think they can raise the money, may be tempted to call in a landscape firm and leave the design and work to them. But research on what children think about their school grounds reinforces the point that the pupils who use the playground must be involved in its physical development, since what adults value may not always be what children want. Wendy Titman (1993) undertook a survey of children's views on school playgrounds. From her evidence, she concluded that school grounds are highly significant for children, yet very few play areas in schools meet their needs. Among the less-liked features of playgrounds are fixed play equipment, murals and playground markings. More liked were features which excited the children's imagination, reducing boredom and challenging their skills: 'natural' features – trees, woods, flowers, shady places; different levels in the grounds; opportunities to climb, hide and explore; and simple items such as formal seating and old tyres.

Sheat and Beer (1994) argue that it is not sufficient just to consult children about playground design – they must be fully involved as partners. Nor is it sufficient to involve children by just asking them what they want; instead, structured activities are needed to elicit their ideas effectively and help the children to feel that their ideas count for something.

The details of playground design go beyond the scope of this book, but the interested reader will find plenty of fascinating ideas in the chapter by Catherine Higgins in Sharp and Smith (1994). Essentially, the advice is to involve a landscape designer only after the children have articulated their needs and wants and, together with the staff and parents, have translated these into an action plan. This takes time, and six stages are outlined.

The first, 'Getting Started', entails deciding who is going to be involved (e.g. professional help, pupils, teaching staff, non-teaching staff, governors, parents, local and voluntary organisations, the local authority); what should be the timescale; and what sources for funds might be tapped. The second stage, 'Gathering Information', essentially involves the pupils, who can be engaged in various kinds of investigative work and reporting. Some of the ideas recommended have been described in the previous section on identifying needs and problems – structured questionnaires on most – and least – liked activities and play areas; giant maps to record how pupils use the grounds, which aspects of it are valued and which cause problems; taking a visitor on a confidential walkabout; or photography work to explain what goes on, where, and the problems this presents for children. Another idea is for the pupils to make a thorough survey of the physical site, its vegetation, topography, microclimate, wildlife, underground services, and so on. The third stage, 'Goal-Setting', again involves the children. For example, possible developments (e.g. a climbing frame, play trails, trees and shrubs, play buildings) are pictorially represented on a series of cards, which children can sort to show their priorities.

It is at the fourth stage, 'Creating Designs', that the landscape designers come in and decisions are made about zones and spaces (e.g. garden area, ball games area, quiet area, water play area), special features, surfaces, and so on. The last two stages are 'Implementing the Designs' and 'Maintenance and Review'. Reassuringly, we are told that schools that have followed these steps have reported significantly fewer playground incidents.

MONITORING AND EVALUATION

Any school which implements the sorts of strategies outlined in this chapter will want to ensure that all the work and money spent has been worthwhile. Once again, a range of personnel can be involved. What do the pupils think? the teachers? the supervisors? parents? governors? Information can be gathered through special measures. One technique is through focused observation of playground behaviour and the use made of any special aspects which have been developed, asking questions such as 'Do children make regular use of the new seating area?', 'Do supervisors observe better behaviour between children', 'Do they experience more respect from the children? Other strategies are administering a questionnaire to pupils and parents, or conducting interviews with samples of them to see if there have been changes in attitudes towards playtimes and lunchtimes. Additionally, data routinely collected, such as the frequency of incidents of playground and behaviour reported to the head, or for which parents have had to be called in, can be analysed. All this may sound like a lot of work, but much can be embedded in the curriculum so that the process of monitoring can be educationally beneficial to the pupils and enhance their social understanding.

CHAPTER 8

Combating Bullying

> Bullying and other forms of harassment can make pupils' lives unhappy, can hinder their academic progress, and can sometimes push otherwise studious children into truancy. In extreme cases it can lead to pupils taking their own lives.
>
> *DfE Circular 8/94, para. 55*

For many children, bullying is the unacceptable face of pupil culture. Often undetected, sometimes condoned by those in authority, it is not only the source of much unhappiness and distress at the time but may continue to mar the victims' lives right into adulthood.

To find out the extent of bullying in urban schools, the initial survey for the Sheffield anti-bullying project asked pupils to complete a questionnaire (Whitney and Smith, 1993). For this purpose, bullying was defined in terms of verbal and indirect actions (whereby victims suffered from 'nasty and unpleasant things' said to them, receiving nasty notes, or no one ever talking to them) as well as physical aggression (being hit, kicked, threatened, locked inside a room). The findings revealed that among a sample of 2,623 pupils in 17 junior and middle schools (the largest primary group in the UK so far researched), 27 per cent reported having been bullied 'sometimes' or more frequently during the current term (mainly by children in their class). As many as 10 per cent reported having being bullied 'once a week' or 'several times a week'. Although the amount of bullying reported by victims varied from school to school, the lowest proportion who said they had been bullied at some time since the beginning of that term was 19 per cent. As far as the perpetrators were concerned, 12 per cent of pupils admitted to having bullied others 'sometimes' or more frequently that term, 4 per cent 'once a week' or 'several times a week'. As children got older, the amount of bullying declined, but individual incidents could still be very serious.

Fortunately, extremely promising findings emerged in a second survey two years later (Whitney *et al.*, 1994). This was based on responses from 2,212 pupils in 16 primary schools (members of a project using a range of measures to combat bullying) and also from a further 99 pupils in a primary school which had not participated in the project. The results were as follows:

Project schools

- The number of victims and the frequency to which they were subjected to bullying had significantly decreased.

- In most schools there were fewer perpetrators of bullying and they bullied less frequently.
- There was a significant increase in pupils reporting that they would not join in bullying others.
- Somewhat more pupils now told adults – especially teachers – if they were being bullied.
- In all schools more pupils now thought that the school was taking action to stop bullying and that that bullying was now less of a problem.
- The effectiveness of the strategies varied from school to school, but the schools which put more effort into their anti-bullying work were correspondingly more effective in reducing bullying.

Comparison school

- Pupils in the primary school which was outside the project responded the least favourably on all the main indicators. Indeed, the amount of bullying there had increased.

In short, the measures taken to combat bullying had been effective, demonstrating once again that schools can make a difference. Given this note of optimism, it is clearly incumbent on all schools to develop anti-bullying policies and intervention strategies.

The main kinds of action which might be taken are summarised in Figure 8.1. It is important to regard an anti-bullying policy as giving rise to a package of strategies so that a multi-pronged approach is adopted. No single measure is likely to make a significant impact since different children have different needs and respond differently to different kinds of strategy. Although no school can be expected to adopt all the main tactics which have proven effective, there should be measures which come within each of the categories in Figure 8.1. Nor should it be thought that all strategies must be agreed before the full policy is established; as soon as any measure has general support, it would seem sensible to implement it.

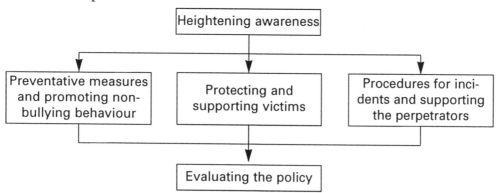

Figure 8.1 Developing a whole-school anti-bullying policy

DEVELOPING A WHOLE-SCHOOL ANTI-BULLYING POLICY

The main features of whole-school behaviour policies in general were discussed in Chapter 6. Clearly it is important for policies on bullying to be included and for the same collaborative steps to be taken as for behaviour in general. This will mean that all adults and pupils in the school plus parents and governors have the opportunity to participate, though obviously the actual drafting will need to be undertaken by a small group. The experience in Sheffield suggests that schools taking shortcuts by not involving everyone are not so successful, while one of the most successful schools used a closure day to invite pupils and parents to discuss its approach (DfE, 1994c). At such a meeting, the opportunity could also be taken to advise parents of the steps they could take to combat bullying (see Kidscape brochure *Stop Bullying!* and DfE, 1994c, part 10, for suggestions and organisations for parents to contact).

The following matters are among those that should be included in a school's anti-bullying policy statement:

- an agreed definition of bullying which makes clear why it is unacceptable, with examples (see 'Raising awareness' below)
- the policy's aims and objectives
- a list of the main preventative measures
- a list of the main measures to protect and support victims
- a list of the procedures for dealing with incidents and helping the perpetrators to change their behaviour and attitude towards bullying
- what pupils and parents should do to report bullying
- how bullying should be monitored and records kept
- how the policy should be evaluated.

With the final statement approved by the governing body, all parents should then be informed of the main aspects of the policy and told where the full statement can be seen. An item on the policy must also be included in the school prospectus.

School governors and staff sometimes fear that such publicity will be counter-productive in broadcasting the message that 'we have bullying at this school'. However, the evidence suggests that such anxieties are misplaced: the message is more likely to be 'we have bullying here like everywhere else, but we're determined to do something about it'. Note that in taking a firm stand against bullying of any kind, it is not so much a question of being 'tough' with bullies as of taking *effective* measures that command the pupils' respect, are seen to protect victims and help the perpetrators to adopt new attitudes towards their behaviour.

Whatever measures are decided upon, the policy needs to be maintained through regular reminders in assembly and by the class teachers and through displays in classrooms and the school entrance. The strategies also need to be carefully monitored, for only then can some objective evidence of their effectiveness be supplied when the policy is subjected to a review. When the policy is set up, therefore, the indicators to assess its effectiveness need to be agreed at that point (see 'Evaluating the policy' below).

HEIGHTENING AWARENESS

When he launched the Department for Education's guidelines on bullying (DfE, 1994c), Eric Forth, the Schools Minister, pointed to the importance of teachers reflecting on the nature and scale of bullying in their school:

> The first hurdle is to acknowledge that the problem exists. It can be difficult for a hard pressed teacher to face up to ... That acknowledgement is a very important one and I am not sure every school has got there yet.

At the outset, it is important that the school community is engaged in two related activities:

- achieving consensus on what sort of behaviour should and should not count as bullying
- appreciating the scale of bullying in the school, given the agreed definition.

What bullying means

Some teachers wonder why much time needs to be spent on arriving at an agreed definition of bullying: why not refer to it simply as unacceptable behaviour? One answer to this is that adults (let alone children) do not behave (let alone believe) as if they agreed about the definition of bullying and its unacceptability: witness the various sorts of pressures and harassment in work places that are sometimes described as 'bullying' but are not so perceived by all the parties involved. In schools, staff may be clear that, say, one child kicking or pushing over another should be counted as bullying. But are they clear whether it is bullying when, say, a child teases another in a jokey way which wasn't meant to hurt but did, or when a group of children do not allow another child to play with them? Even if the teaching staff are agreed about the meaning of bullying, the playground supervisors and children may have different perceptions. All staff and pupils therefore need to share their understandings about what specific target behaviours they consider need addressing and why the behaviours are unacceptable. It is also important for this definition to be discussed among the parents (some of whom may effectively be condoning some of the behaviours the staff want to stop). Their cooperation is essential if the problem is to be effectively tackled on all fronts.

The Sheffield Project used a definition of bullying that children could easily understand:

> We say a child or young person is being bullied, or picked on, when another child or young person, or a group of children or young people, say nasty and unpleasant things to him or her. It is also bullying when a child or young person is hit, kicked, threatened, locked inside a room, sent nasty notes, when no one ever talks to them and things like that. These things can happen frequently and it is difficult for the child or young person being bullied to defend himself or herself. It is also bullying when a pupil is teased repeatedly in a nasty way.
>
> But it is not bullying when two children or young people of about the same strength have the odd fight or quarrel.
>
> (Smith and Sharp, 1994, p.13)

As the above definition makes clear, bullying is unacceptable because it is an *abuse of power* – it involves the *'dominance* of one pupil by another, or a group of others' (DfE 1994a, para.55, emphasis added). Where this is clearly absent, the action does not count as bullying: examples are the odd fight between two pupils of similar strength and stamina, engagement in 'rough and tumble' rather than aggressive play, or the occasional friendly tease that causes laughter but not hurt. None of these count as bullying since there is not what Olweus (1993) has referred to as an asymmetric relationship of power, making the victim feel hurt, isolated, rejected, friendless or lonely.

One way of preparing for a discussion on the meaning of bullying is to ask pupils to write or draw about, say, their playground experiences or to list the things they like and dislike about school. The teacher can then use this work to engage the class in general discussion about incidents that might and might not be properly referred to as bullying. Alternatively, the teacher could prepare short scenarios (e.g. 'Darren keeps calling Sarah a sissy when she is frightened to swim at the deep end of the baths', or 'Tracy is upset because some girls in her class won't let her play with them', or 'Paul and John wrestled on the classroom floor and then got up laughing'). Pupils in groups are then asked to discuss each scenario and say whether the behaviour depicted amounts to bullying and how they should respond if they were victims or witnessed it. (For more suggested scenarios, see Sharp and Thompson, 1994). Activities such as these should not only help to increase understanding of the concept but also help to engender an ethos of openness so that pupils do not suffer in silence. It is important, however, to preserve confidentiality in order that individual children are not made to feel embarrassed or victimised by having their unpleasant experiences discussed in public.

The examples given in Figure 8.2 indicate the range of actions that could be included as examples of bullying behaviour. The five categories suggested recognise that there are various types of bullying – psychological as well as physical – and that bullying can sometimes be indirect, as when a child is ignored by another or a group, or when pupils effectively condone bullying by watching it and taking no remedial action. It is important that pupils appreciate the different dimensions of bullying so that the full range of distressing situations that arise from another's dominance can be addressed. The Sheffield Project, for instance, found that most bullying took the form of name-calling, with being hit or threatened coming second. But there were significant gender differences: while boys were more likely to be physically hit and threatened, girls were more likely to suffer from direct verbal bullying, having rumours spread about them, or being ostracised. The idea that 'sticks and stones will break my bones but words will never hurt me' is patently untrue. More boys than girls admitted to bullying others in one way or another, but only slightly more boys reported experiences of being bullied.

Physical
hitting
kicking
pulling hair
punching
shoving or tripping up
damaging belongings
assaulting with a
  weapon

Passive
being a bystander

Direct Verbal
name-calling
mocking someone's
  appearance or speech
abusive or offensive
  remarks
racial or sexual
  harassment
hurtful teasing
jeering
intimidation
extortion

Indirect
spreading spiteful stories
passing nasty notes
exclusion from peer
  group

Gestural
making faces or abusive
  signs
showing hostility
ignoring
rejecting

Figure 8.2 Examples of bullying behaviour

The Sheffield study also showed that whereas boys were more likely to be bullied by other boys than by girls, girls said they were bullied by boys as well as by other girls. Everyday experience would suggest that bullying of girls by boys as well as by other girls seems to consist largely of references to appearance and, for older girls, to sexual reputation. Whereas boys tend to regard bullying other boys as about being macho, girls seem to bully other girls for motives of jealousy, often associated with the victim's prettiness or attractiveness. Girls' friendship patterns also seem to be more volatile than boys', with close relationships one day being replaced by ostracising the next.

In discussing the meaning of bullying with their classes, teachers may find that children do not always accept adults' perceptions of the nature of bullying. Some writers, for instance, assume that bullying behaviour necessarily involves aggressiveness and that it is both intentional and long-standing. For example, Smith and Thompson (1991, p.1) state that bullying 'can be taken to be a subset of aggressive behaviour', while the DfE pack states that bullying 'is deliberately hurtful behaviour' and that 'it is repeated over a period of time'

(DfE, 1994c, para 1.8). However, the experience of the confidential phone service Childline is that from the *victim's* point of view these conditions do not always apply (La Fontaine, 1991). Many callers have been seriously upset by isolated incidents, or by mild teasing which may not have been designed to hurt so much as to attract admiration or laughter from other children – but it became distressing over time. Again, among callers who wanted to talk about intentional actions, the behaviour they described was not always 'aggressiveness', at least as it is conventionally understood, but simply words or conduct which conveyed the message 'I want to reject you' or 'I'm hostile to you'. In short, victims seemed to define bullying more in terms of its *effects* than its permanence, intentionality or aggressiveness. It may be, too, that this phenomenon applies particularly to girls, who may be more ready to regard being excluded or rejected as 'bullying' when they are the victims than when they perpetrate such behaviour themselves (Siann, *et al.*, 1994).

This discussion about the meaning of bullying is not just about semantics. For it is part of children's social education to realise that the effects of their actions may have unintended consequences, whatever the underlying intentions, and that considerate behaviour involves predicting the consequences of what you say or do (or don't say or do). Obviously no teacher should describe as a bully a child whose actions were not intended to hurt; none the less, children need to know when their actions upset others and may be *perceived* as bullying behaviour, and they need to develop a style of behaving that does not unwittingly inflict distress on other more vulnerable children, both for the sake of their own popularity as well as for the pupil who is troubled. Otherwise they will grow into adults who seem to cause tension and are generally regarded as wanting to hold power over others.

Gathering data

Once pupils understand more of the nature of bullying, the next step is to ascertain how prevalent it is. Teachers are often unaware about the extent of bullying or of all the forms it takes, partly because those at the receiving end are often too frightened or embarrassed to say anything, and partly because many incidents occur away from staff supervision. There is much to be said for administering a questionnaire, not necessarily to the whole school but to, say, Years 5 and 6. This can be a rather time-consuming exercise, and care needs to be taken over the wording of questions to ensure that the intended meaning is conveyed and that children with reading problems can participate. For a comprehensive survey that explores all aspects of bullying, it is best to use one of the published measures to maximise the probability that the results will be valid and reliable (see Sharp, Arora, Smith and Whitney, 1994) This will also make it possible to compare the results with those from other schools using the same measure.

If instead it is decided to develop a questionnaire in-house, then it is vital to take the precautions recommended in the Department for Education's guidelines (DfE, 1994c, paras 3.8–11). However, schools could easily use the simple survey technique recommended by Sharp, Arora, Smith and Whitney (1994). At the end of a mid-day break, pupils are given a list of bullying behaviours and asked (without giving their names) to place a tick in one of three columns to indicate whether during that lunchtime the behaviour did not happen to them, happened once, or happened more than once.

After the questionnaire responses have been collated, pupils can make charts and diagrams to display the results, which in turn can be used to generate discussion in the classroom, assembly and amongst the adults in the school community. This exercise should ensure that teachers and others do not underestimate the scale of the problem, nor exaggerate it, and that everybody is clear just what kinds of bullying behaviour need addressing and in which locations special action needs to be taken. The findings will also provide base-line material for any follow-up survey to evaluate the measures used to reduce bullying.

PREVENTATIVE MEASURES AND PROMOTING NON-BULLYING BEHAVIOUR

Prevention is at the heart of any anti-bullying policy. It can be taken at a number of levels, as shown in Checklist 8.1. Many of the suggestions have been discussed in previous chapters: praise and rewards for pro-social behaviour in Chapter 3; enhancing self-esteem and teaching cooperative games in Chapter 4; setting up a school council in Chapter 5; and playground policies in Chapter 7. The latter is particularly important since about three-quarters of bullying incidents occur in the playground (DfE, 1994c). For both the playground and other occasions, many schools find it helpful to 'twin' newcomers with older pupils, who are encouraged to befriend and look after them.

Much preventative work can be achieved at classroom level. At the very least, schools can ensure that rules to combat bullying are included in its codes of behaviour. Examples might be promises not to bully other pupils, to help any who are bullied, and to include pupils who may easily be left out (Olweus, 1993).

More specifically, it is important for teachers to give children plenty of practice in producing non-aggressive solutions to potentially aggressive situations. In an Australian study (Slee, 1993), primary school children who engaged in bullying, or were victims, produced significantly fewer solutions to hypothetical aggressive acts than did other children. Moreover, although all the children chose a non-aggressive response as their first solution, bullies were significantly more likely to choose an aggressive response as their second-best solution. The suggestion is that schools should encourage children to develop social skills in offering non-aggressive but effective responses to situations involving interpersonal conflict. For practical ideas here, the reader is referred to the 'What ifs?' exercises provided in the Kidscape booklet *Stop Bullying*.

Checklist 8.1
Preventative measures for combating bullying

General school arrangements	✓ Rewards for co-operative and altruistic behaviour ✓ Plenty of extra-curricular opportunities ✓ School Council
Classroom & assembly	✓ Being sensitive to the possibility of teacher-bullying ✓ Formulating rules to combat bullying ✓ Measures to enhance self-esteem ✓ Quality Circles
Lunchtime and playground level	✓ Effective playground supervision ✓ Playground code ✓ Playground design ✓ Attention to play facilities and equipment ✓ Plenty to do during break periods
Home-school liaison	✓ Regular items in newsletters ✓ Special meetings and discussion groups with parents

---

The strategy known as *Quality Circles* (QCs) is a particularly valuable one for children who already have had experience of circle-time or collaborative group work (Chapter 4). Adapted from industry for use in the Sheffield Project, QCs enable virtually every child in a class to become involved in generating measures to combat bullying. Like no other strategy, QCs give pupils a sense of ownership of school policy since they are in keeping with a participative management model. Through a series of steps over a number of sessions, small groups of pupils identify problems, analyse their causes and develop solutions which they present to the school's senior management team. Although QCs in schools were developed to combat bullying, they can be used to to address any issue that relates to whether the school is a pleasant place to live and work in, so the potential is considerable.

The steps involved have been fully described by Cowie and Sharp (1994a and 1994b), and the reader is urged to read these detailed accounts before attempting to implement the strategy. However, the summary below gives a flavour of what is involved:

Stage 1: Introduction. The teacher explains to the class that the pupils are to be given the opportunity to put forward ideas on how to tackle bullying behaviour. The class is then divided into groups of five to eight children (the younger the pupils, the smaller the group). Each Quality Circle gives itself a name (and perhaps makes a shield to promote group identity) and appoints a chairperson and a recorder.

Stage 2: Identifying the problems. The chairperson of each QC engages the group in brainstorming to identify possible topics which members think need addressing, and the recorder makes a list. The ideas are accepted without judgements being made. After a stated period of time the suggestions are pooled by the teacher, and the class then discusses them and decides which issue it wants to address first. The teacher may want to encourage the pupils to take something pretty straightforward at the start so that they can experience success without undue difficulty to begin with. (Whether all the QCs take the same problem or different ones is also a matter for decision, but the former is probably easier to manage and gives opportunity for groups to compare their conclusions.)

Stage 3: Analysing the problem. Each QC discusses why the problem exists, and records the ideas expressed. The job of the chairperson is to encourage fluency and chains of ideas by calling out 'Why?' when suggestions are made. The responses are listed by the recorder, perhaps as a flow chart. It may be appropriate to conduct surveys on some matters to generate data about some of the points raised, for example on the nature of playground behaviour. The teacher can again pool ideas, on the basis of which the QCs decide what causal factor should be addressed first. Here the teacher may want to encourage the groups to be realistic and go for something not too complicated. For example, if the problem under discussion was name-calling and one causal suggestion was 'their Mum and Dad set a bad example', it would probably not be sensible to try to address this directly! But if another suggestion was 'some kids just imitate others', then that could be tackled.

Stage 4: Developing a solution. The group then sets about suggesting ways of addressing the factor identified for action at the end of Stage 3. Again, the chairperson encourages as many ideas as possible, this time repeating the question 'How?'. This serves to ensure that each suggestion is fully explored. The recorder notes down all the ideas, after which the group decides which one(s) to develop further. (Again, groups must be realistic). The QCs develop and refine their solutions to produce a workable strategy.

Stage 5: Presenting ideas to management. This is a very important stage in the process. If senior staff sound dismissive of ideas they don't agree with, the whole exercise will fall flat on its face and pupil morale will suffer. The management team should therefore set aside a time to receive the QC's presentation, listen to it attentively, make positive comments, and agree a time when the group meets again. At this second meeting, management should list the pros and cons of the proposal, and then give its considered view. It is obviously very important that the QC does not feel discouraged by any negative response. If the staff feel that the suggestions should not be implemented in part or at all, they must state their reasons and give support to the QC to think up new ideas.

Stage 6: Taking it further. The QC meets again to discuss management's response and takes the matter from there, either implementing the proposal (probably with staff help) or making changes. If necessary more meetings can be arranged with the management team.

PROTECTING AND SUPPORTING VICTIMS

An anti-bullying policy must not only set up strategies that help victims to feel safe: it must reassure those who are bullied that adults in the school will listen to what they say and take action. Reporting that you have been bullied must never be construed as 'sneaking'. The unmistakable message must be 'It's OK to tell', and this should be regularly reinforced by class teachers, in assembly and in newsletters to parents.

There are a number of reasons why victims often keep their experiences of bullying to themselves. There is the fear of reprisals; the fear that adults will not welcome 'telling tales' and have little patience with individuals who can't stand up for themselves; the fear that even a sympathetic adult will take no action or will be satisfied with the perpetrator's plea that 'it was only in fun'; the fear that they may be accused of 'bringing it on' themselves; and just feelings of confusion, distress, and helplessness. So not only must there be clear guidelines for pupils, staff and parents to report bullying: it is also important that teachers and parents should be encouraged to watch out for signs of bullying – for example, wanting to stay away from school, being withdrawn, complaining of tummy aches or not eating or sleeping, having property missing or unexplained bruises and cuts (Elliott, 1991).

Checklist 8.2 lists possible strategies by which victims or potential victims can receive reassurance and support both directly and indirectly. A suitable handout given to children (or their parents) when joining the school can help to convey the message that the staff wants to address the problem of bullying; it can also describe the steps that a pupil or parent should take to report any incident. An example of an imaginative leaflet produced by one school is given in Figure 8.3. Note how the illustrations and presentation, as well as the content, help the reader to believe that the school is a caring community and that pupils will not be subjected to feelings of isolation.

> **Checklist 8.2**
> **Protection and support for victims**
>
> *Direct measures* ✓ It's OK to tell
> ✓ Clear and well-publicised procedures for reporting incidents
> ✓ Everyone taking incidents seriously
> ✓ Special leaflet for new pupils (see Fig 8.3)
> ✓ Named persons as counsellors
> ✓ Curriculum provision for enhancing self-confidence and skills in assertiveness
> ✓ Teachers and parents being alert to signs of bullying
>
> *Indirect measures* ✓ Role-play and discussion based on everyday scenarios
> ✓ Literature and videos to stimulate discussion

Apart from trying to ensure a climate of openness, where children know that incidents will be taken seriously, it can be helpful to have named members of staff who act as counsellors. This does not mean that pupils are discouraged from reporting bullying to anyone else, such as their class teacher or parent, but it does enable pupils to know that there are particular teachers who have volunteered to offer help and advice in confidence. Advice for self-protection might include sticking with a group, leaving expensive possessions at home and acting assertively but not aggressively. Assertiveness training to build up a victim's confidence can also be provided, but is best made available to all children to avoid stigmatisation. Vulnerable pupils can thus acquire strategies both to avoid being bullied and to deal effectively but non-aggressively with bullying behaviour, depriving bullies of the response they find rewarding. Indeed, some schools have found it helpful to set up lunchtime or after-school clubs in assertiveness for any pupil who cares to come along. At these sessions, pupils can be given practice in, for instance, ignoring or laughing off hurtful remarks, in assertively saying 'No' and walking away confidently with head high, and taking long strides and looking straight ahead (see Arora, 1991, for an account of the work of victim support groups).

Pupils who experience bullying, or who are afraid that they might do so, can also be helped indirectly. Here, role play and drama have unique value in allowing children to work through their emotions in a safe setting. Probably no other strategy so effectively enables pupils to encounter the feelings of being a victim, bystander or bully, to appreciate the consequences of bullying, to

1. Q. WHAT IS BULLYING?
A. WORDS OR ACTIONS INTENDED TO HURT.

2. BULLYING CAN BE:-
PHYSICAL — Hitting
— Kicking
— Punching
— Biting
— Pinching
OR ANY ACTION INTENDED TO HURT.

3. BULLIES CAN USE WORDS TO TEASE ABOUT SOMEONE'S:
— Shape
— Colour
— Looks
— Intelligence
— Skills
— Nationality

4. BULLIES CAN USE WORDS TO SCARE:
by Shouting or Threatening

5. BULLIES EXCLUDE PEOPLE AND ENCOURAGE OTHERS TO DO THE SAME:
They leave people out of games, refuse to share a book or a seat, refuse to clean a plate or lend a pencil.
DELIBERATELY IGNORING SOMEONE CAN BE BULLYING.

6. HOW DO BULLIES ACT?
— Sometimes alone, sometimes in groups. Bullies often get others to do their bullying for them, they have the ideas but don't want to be caught bullying.

7. WHAT DO BULLIES LOOK LIKE?
They come in all shapes and sizes, all ages, boys and girls, men and women. Bullies are not always obvious. Sometimes they appear to be popular. Bullies like having power over people.

8. WHAT DO I DO IF I SEE SOMEONE BEING BULLIED?
Support them—don't only support your friends or class, support all victims, even those you may not like. You know that bullying is wrong.

9. HOW DO I SUPPORT SOMEONE?
Seek the help of an adult, and show the victim kindness. Stick up for them. Point out to the bully that it is bullying.

10. DON'T IGNORE BULLYING BECAUSE IT DOES NOT INVOLVE YOU.
Don't enjoy bullying. Watching someone being bullied and enjoying it is much the same as bullying someone.

Figure 8.3 A leaflet distributed to all pupils at Hoe School

experiment in making different kinds of response to incidents and to develop personal skills in dealing with bullying incidents. It is easier in role-play for children to express their destructive, ambivalent and positive feelings without taking the risks that real-life situations present. At first, the teacher will need to suggest scenarios, but after such initial experience pupils can devise their own incidents. For more examples and advice, see Cowie and Sharp (1994a, b).

Like role-play, literature and videos provide a means for children to address their personal relationship problems without having to make public their own distressing experiences. Through a story or a film, children can confront their problems and explore possible responses to bullying behaviour. For instance, in *The Bully* by Jan Needle (Hamish Hamilton, 1994), a victim called Simon is tormented by two girls; unfortunately, Simon is known to the staff as a liar and is sometimes found throwing stones at his alleged tormenter. Here is the kind of problematic situation which many children and teachers will recognise: the victim's own behaviour is not exactly exemplary, and the staff are not adept at getting at the truth of the alleged bullying. Lists of suitable books and videos for children which deal with bullying are given in Elliott (1991), Sharp and Smith (1994) and Tattum and Herbert (1990).

It must be stressed that protective measures should not be designed to put the onus for stopping bullying on the children who are most vulnerable. Supporting victims and potential victims is complementary to, not a substitute for, addressing the incidents themselves and dealing with the perpetrators, a matter to which we now turn.

PROCEDURES FOR INCIDENTS AND SUPPORTING THE PERPETRATORS

The way to deal with offenders is probably the most difficult aspect of an anti-bullying policy, but for this reason needs special attention in the school's policy to combat bullying. The general principle is to take action which makes an unequivocal stand whilst also being constructive and not driving the culprit to 'take it out' on the victim. Sufferers often bear their agony in secret because of this fear. A summary of the kind of strategies that need to be considered is given in Checklist 8.3.

As part of a survey on bullying among primary school children, Boulton and Underwood (1992) asked 22 of the 8- to 10-year-olds who admitted they had bullied other pupils how they felt when they engaged in this behaviour. About a quarter said that they did so because it made them feel good about themselves. This finding suggests that the objective in dealing with perpetrators of bullying must be not so much to confront the bully with his or her behaviour but to take steps to stop the bullying by encouraging a change of attitude. In cases of group bullying among children mainly of nine years upwards, the Sheffield Project

> **Checklist 8.3**
> **Procedures for incidents and supporting the perpetrators**
>
> ✓ Clear and effective arrangements for interviewing those involved (e.g. the No Blame Approach or the Method of Shared Concern) and monitoring progress
> ✓ Clear methods for recording incidents
> ✓ Reinforcing the attempts of perpetrators to realise success in acceptable pursuits
> ✓ Procedures for informing parents of perpetrators and victims
> ✓ Encouraging parents of children who bully to help them find success in positive activities

found the Method of Common Concern (which it renamed the Method of Shared Concern), to be often effective in finding a solution which enables victim and perpetrators to live with each other (Sharp, Cowie and Smith, 1994). This is a counselling-based approach developed by Anatol Pikas in Sweden. An alternative procedure which many schools are now adopting is the No Blame Approach developed by Barbara Maines and George Robinson (1992).

As can be seen from the summaries in Figure 8.4, the two procedures have much in common:

- The underlying assumption is that the onus to stop the bullying must not be on the victim. All children can be helped to develop the social skills needed to deal with bullying and to prevent provoking incidents, and victims presenting maladaptive behaviours should be given specialist help; but once bullying takes place, it must be dealt with by encouraging the perpetrators and others condoning the action to share responsibility for stopping it.
- A teacher acts upon information of a bullying incident, defined in terms of verbal bullying, threats and ostracising as well as physical aggression.
- A series of interviews is arranged with all involved, the aim being to stop the bullying by creating an ethos of shared responsibility amongst those responsible. The supposition is that such intervention should address the problems of peer pressure among the perpetrators.
- Details of the incident or its causes are not discussed lest these deflect from the main aim.
- Attributions of blame or punishment do not enter into the procedures except for serious assault. 'We take a pragmatic approach and suggest that punishment simply does not work; in fact it will often make things worse when the bully takes further revenge on the victim' (Maines and Robinson, 1992, p.7).

The Method of Shared Concern
(Pikas, 1989, developed by Sharp, Cowie and Smith, 1994)

1. In a quiet room, where privacy can be ensured, and without forewarning, the teacher first meets the perpetrator and bystanders individually for 7–10 minutes each (but without a break). The interviews, which are non-confrontation and do not attribute blame, start with the person who holds most power in the group and use a special script. For each individual, the teacher:
   - says 'I hear you have been nasty to X. Tell me about it'. The particulars of the incident are not negotiated.
   - asks for agreement that 'X is having a bad time in school';
   - invites suggestions 'to help X in this situation', and encourages the ideas to be put into practice;
   - arranges to meet again in a week's time.

2. The victim is then interviewed, with the teacher adopting a counselling role and discussing how to address any matters that might provoke bullying.

3. Once the victim is ready to meet the group, a follow-up meeting is arranged. Praise is given if the bullying is stopped, or support is given to individuals to re-work the solution.

4. Some time later, another group meeting is arranged, first with the perpetrators to review progress and make positive statements about the victim. The victim then joins the group, to whom the pupils repeat their positive statements and discuss what to do should anyone start the bullying again. Long -term agreement is then established through discussion about ideas such as learning to live together.

5. The group might meet again, but in any case the teacher makes a follow-up investigation after a few weeks.

The No Blame Approach
(Maines and Robinson, 1992)

1. The first interview is with the victim, who is invited to:
   - tell about his/her feelings and to express them through a poem or a picture;
   - indicate who is involved (but not the details of the incident).

2. The perpetrators and some bystanders are seen as a group. The teacher
   - relates the victim's feelings, using the poem/picture but does not discuss details of the incident, or ask why the individuals have bullied, or attribute blame;
   - asks each individual for a suggestion to make the victim feel happier, giving positive responses but without extracting promises of changed behaviour;
   - gives the group the responsibility to solve the problem.

3. A week later, the teacher monitors the situation by meeting the group again and discussing with each child, including the victim, how matters have progressed.

Figure 8.4 Interviewing procedures for dealing with bullying incidents

However, there are a number of differences between the two approaches:

- Pikas (1989) argues that his method is suitable for group bullying situations ('mobbing'), but for one-to-one bullying and for children below nine it is appropriate to adopt a firm stance and insist the bullying stops. In contrast, Maines and Robinson (1992) make no such distinction. They argue that even if there appears to be only one bully, there is more than likely to be onlookers who effectively condone the situation and should therefore share responsibility for its resolution.
- For the Method of Shared Concern, teachers are advised to stick to a special script (see Sharp, Cowie and Smith, 1994). For the No Blame Approach more general guidance is given.
- In the No Blame Approach, the victim is interviewed first so that his/her feelings can be relayed to the perpetrators. In the Method of Shared Concern the victim is interviewed only after the meeting of those responsible, the argument being that he or she is then protected from further abuse as a result of 'telling tales'.
- In the Method of Shared Concern, the perpetrators are interviewed one by one. In the No Blame Approach, they are seen as a group so that those reluctant to address the issue will be encouraged when they witness positive responses from others.

In deciding whether to adopt either of these approaches, schools can be reassured by the claims of success for both, though the evidence is based largely on case studies produced by the adherents rather than on independent evaluations. If the procedures do not produce a satisfactory solution for an incident, other action will be necessary, such as involving the parents, ensuring that members of bullying gangs do not remain in the same class, or developing individual behaviour plans for the perpetrators (see Chapter 5).

EVALUATING THE POLICY

Once a year it is important for the school to review its anti-bullying policy. This might be done by a governors' sub-committee that includes teacher and parent governors. There are three main sorts of question that might be asked:

- *Have there actually been fewer incidents of bullying?* (This will mean keeping a log of incidents and asking mid-day supervisors for their comments.)
- *Do pupils believe there is less bullying going on*, that they are able to tell staff about incidents, and that the school is trying to stop bullying? (This will mean administering a simple questionnaire to, say, one or two year groups.)
- *What is the teaching staff's experience of the particular strategies* that have been used? Should these remain or be changed or added to?

Of course, if pupils feel more able to tell adults about what is going on, one might expect the number of reported incidents to increase. A true indication of changes in bullying behaviour will therefore not be apparent until the greater feeling of openness has become established.

There is always the danger that, in its determination to stamp out bullying, a school will adopt an over-earnest approach which engenders feelings of guilt without empowering the more vulnerable pupils. Work in prevention and support for both victims and perpetrators should generate creative enterprise and fun. In that way the bullying culture is deprived of the ethos in which it thrives and the community is more likely to grow in mutual respect.

Further Reading

CLASSROOM MANAGEMENT AND DISCIPLINE

Charlton, T. and David, K. (1993) (eds) *Managing Misbehaviour in Schools*. London: Routledge.

McManus, M. (1995) *Troublesome Behaviour in the Classroom: Meeting Individual Needs*. London: Routledge.

Munn, P., Johnstone, M. and Chalmers, V. (1992) *Effective Discipline in Primary Schools and Classrooms*. London: Chapman.

Neill, S. and Caswell, C. (1993) *Body Language for Competent Teachers*. London: Routledge.

Rogers, W.A. (1994) *The Language of Discipline*. Plymouth: Northcote House.
(Besides much useful general comment on encouraging children and dealing with behaviour problems, this book focuses interestingly on the efficacy of different kinds of teachers' remarks.)

Wragg, E.C. (1993) *Class Management*. London: Routledge. (Based on the Leverhulme Project)

EMOTIONAL AND BEHAVIOURAL DIFFICULTIES

Chazan, M., Laing, A. and Davies, D. (1994) *Emotional and Behavioural Difficulties in Middle Childhood*. Basingstoke: Falmer Press.

Cooper, P., Smith, C.J. and Upton, G. (1994) *Emotional and Behavioural Difficulties*. London: Routledge.

Gray, P., Miller, A. and Noakes, J. (eds)(1994) *Challenging Behaviour in Schools*. London: Routledge.

Green, C. (1995) *Understanding Attention Deficit Disorder*. London: Vermilion.

Hinshaw, S.P. (1994) *Attention Deficits and Hyperactivity in Children*. Thousand Oaks: Sage.

Leeds Education Authority (1992). *Managing the Difficult to Manage*. Positive Behaviour Service, West Park Curriculum Development Centre, Spen Lane, Leeds LS16 5BB.

Train, A. (1993) *Helping the Aggressive Child*. London: Souvenir Press.

SELF-ESTEEM, COOPERATIVE LEARNING AND BUILDING A COMMUNITY ETHOS

Bliss, T. and Tetley, J. (1993; 1995) *Circle Time* and *Developing Circle Time*. Bristol: Lame Duck. A video, *Coming Round to Circle Time*, is also available.

Borba, M. and Borba, C. (1980; 1982) *Self-esteem: A Classroom Affair*, Vols. 1 and 2. San Francisco: Harper.

Gibbs, J. (1978) *Tribes: A Process for Social Development and Cooperative Learning*. Santa Rosa: Center Source Publications. (A manual of material to develop self-esteem and social cohesion in the school community.)

Jenkin, F. (1989) *Making Small Groups Work*. Oxford: Penguin Educational.

Kagan, S. (1989) *Cooperative Learning: Resources for Teachers*. San Juan Capistrano: Resources for Teachers.

Mosley, J. (1994) *Turn Your School Around*. Wisbech, Cambs: Learning Development Aids.

Roberts, R. (1995) *Self-esteem and Successful Early Learning*. Sevenoaks: Hodder & Stoughton.

Slavin, R.E. (1990) *Cooperative Learning*. Boston: Allyn and Bacon.

WHOLE-SCHOOL BEHAVIOUR POLICY

Allen, B. (1994) *Behaviour* (Series: It Makes My Life Easier). Bristol: Lame Duck Publishing.

Leeds Education Authority (1994) *Developing a Behaviour Policy and Putting it into Practice*. Positive Behaviour Service, West Park Curriculum Development Centre, Spen Lane, Leeds LS16 5BB.

School Council Starter Pack. School Councils U.K., 57 Etchingham Park Road, London N3 2EB. 0181-349 2459.

Thompson, D. and Sharp, S. (1994) *Improving Schools: Establishing and Integrating Whole School Behaviour Policies*. London: David Fulton.

PLAYGROUND AND LUNCHTIME POLICY

Blatchford, P. and Sharp, S. (eds) *Breaktime and the School: Understanding and Changing Playground Behaviour*. London: Routledge.

Ross, C. and Ryan, A. (1990) *Can I Stay In Today, Miss?* Stoke on Trent: Trentham Books.

Titman, W. (1994) *Special Places, Special People*. Godalming: World Wide Fund for Nature.

There are also relevant chapters in the books edited by Sharp and Smith (see next section).

Advice addressed specifically to supervisors

OPTIS (1986) *Lunchtime Supervision*. Oxford: Optis House.

Additionally, there are now a number of training packages for midday supervisors, including:

Hayley, J. and Metcalf, C. (1993) *Lunchbox* (trainer pack for supervisors). Obtainable from White House Unit, Salthouse Road, Hull HU8 9HJ.

Leeds Education Authority (1994) *The Lunch Pack*. Positive Behaviour Service, West Park Curriculum Development Centre, Spen Lane, Leeds LS16 5BB.

Walsall Educational Development Centre (1995) *Training Manual for Lunchtime Supervisors*. Centre at Field Road, Bloxwich, Walsall WS3 3JF. The pack includes the video *395 to Lunch: Managing at Midday*, produced by the National Primary Centre.

Waltham Forest Education Department (1993) *Breaking for Lunch* (video and manual). Client Division, Leyton, Municipal Offices, High Street, London E10 5QJ.

BULLYING POLICY

Department for Education (1994) *Bullying: Don't Suffer in Silence*.

Leeds Education Authority (1994) *Say No to Bullying*. Positive Behaviour Service, West Park Curriculum Development Centre, Spen Lane, Leeds LS16 5BB.

Maines, B. and Robinson, G. (1994) *Bullying* (on developing policy), *Stamp Out Bullying* (strategies for combating bullying) and *The No Blame Approach* (on responding to bullying incidents). (Series: It Makes My Life Easier) Bristol: Lame Duck.

Sharp, S. and Smith, P.K. (eds) (1994) *Tackling Bullying in Your School*. London: Routledge. (Contains a detailed list of resources, including books for children and parents and particulars of organisations.)

Smith, P.K. and Sharp, S. (eds) (1994) *School Bullying: Insights and Perspectives*. London: Routledge.

Tattum, D.P. (ed)(1993) *Understanding and Managing Bullying*. London: Heinemann.

References

Alexander, R. (1992) *Policy and Practice in Primary Education*. London: Routledge.

Alexander, R., Rose, J. and Woodhead, C. (1992) *Curriculum Organisation and Classroom Practice in Primary Schools*. London: Department of Education and Science.

Andrews, C. and Hinton, S. (1991) *Enhancing the Quality of Play in School Playgrounds*. London: National Children's Play and Recreation Unit.

Arnstein, S.R. (1969) 'A ladder of citizen participation'. *AIP Journal*, July, 216–24.

Aronfreed, J. (1976) 'Moral development from the standpoint of a general psychological theory'. In T. Lickona (ed) *Moral Development and Behaviour*. New York: Holt, Rinehart & Winston.

Arora, T. (1991) 'The use of victim support groups'. In P.K.Smith and D. Thompson (eds) *Practical Approaches to Bullying*. London: David Fulton.

Bain, A., Houghton, S. and Williams, S. (1991) 'The effects of a school-wide behaviour management programme on teachers' use of encouragement in the classroom', *Educational Studies*, 17, 249–60.

Barker, G.P. and Graham, S. (1987) 'Developmental study of praise and blame as attributional cues'. *Journal of Educational Psychology*, 79, 62–66.

Bar-Tal, D. (1984) 'The effects of teachers' behaviour on pupils' attributions: a review'. In P. Barnes, J. Oates, J. Chapman, V. Lee and P. Czerniewska (eds) *Personality, Development and Learning*. Sevenoaks: Hodder and Stoughton.

Bennett, N., Desforges, C. Cockburn, A. and Wilkinson, B. (1984) *The Quality of Pupil Learning Experiences*. Hillsdale: Erlbaum.

Bennett, S.N. and Dunne, E. (1992) *Managing Classroom Groups*. Hemel Hempstead: Simon and Shuster.

Blatchford, P. (1989) *Playtime in the Primary School: Problems and Improvements*. Windsor: NFER-Nelson.

Blatchford, P., Creeser, R. and Mooney, A, (1990) 'Playground games and playtime: the children's view', *Educational Research*, 32, 163–74.

Blatchford, P. and Sharp. (1994) 'Why understand and why change school breaktime behaviour?' In P. Blatchford and S. Sharp (eds), *Breaktime and the School: Understanding and Changing Playground Behaviour*. London: Routledge.

Bliss, T. and Tetley, J. (1993; 1995) *Circle Time* and *Developing Circle Time*. Bristol: Lame Duck Publishing

Boulton, M.J. (1994a) ' Playful and aggressive fighting in the middle-school playground'. In P. Blatchford, and S. Sharp, (eds) *Breaktime and the School: Understanding and Changing Playground Behaviour*. London: Routledge.

Boulton, M.J. (1994b) 'Understanding and preventing bullying in the junior school playground'. In P.K. Smith and S. Sharp (eds) *School Bullying: Insights and Perspectives*. London: Routledge.

Boulton, M.J. (1994c) 'How to prevent and respond to bullying behaviour in the junior/middle school playground'. In S. Sharp and P.K. Smith (eds) *Tackling Bullying in Your School: A Practical Handbook for Teachers*. London: Routledge.

Boulton, M. and Underwood, K. (1992) 'Bully/victim problems among middle school children'. *British Journal of Educational Psychology*, 62, 73–87.

Brading, R. (1989) School Councils in Primary Schools. Unpublished MA dissertation, Roehampton Institute London.

Brattesani, K., Weinstein, R.S. and Marshall, H.H. (1984) 'Student perceptions of differential teacher treatment as moderators of teacher expectation effects'. *Journal of Educational*

Psychology, 76, 236–47.

Brophy, J. (1981) 'Teacher praise: a functional analysis'. *Review of Educational Research*, 15, 5–32.

Brophy, J. (1983) 'Research on the self-fulfilling prophecy and teacher expectations'. *Journal of Educational Psychology*, 75, 631–61.

Burgner, D. and Hewstone, M. (1993) 'Young children's causal attributions for success and failure: "self-enhancing" boys and "self-derogating" girls'. *British Journal of Educational Psychology*, 11, 125–29.

Canter, L. and Canter, M. (1992) *Assertive Discipline: Positive Behaviour Management for Today's Classroom*. Santa Monica: Lee Canter Associates.

Central Advisory Council for Education (1976) *Children and Their Primary Schools*. Plowden Report, Volume 1. London: HMSO.

Chambers, B. (1993) 'Cooperative learning in kindergarten: can it enhance students' prosocial behaviour?. *International Journal of Early Childhood*, 25, 31–6.

Cohen, E. (1986) *Designing Groupwork*. New York: Teachers College Press.

Cooper, H.M. and Tom, D.Y.H. (1984) 'Teacher expectation research: a review with implications for classroom instruction'. *Elementary School Journal*, 85, 77–89.

Coopersmith, J. (1967) *The Antecedents of Self-esteem*. San Fransisco: Freeman.

Coulby, J. and Coulby, D. (1990) 'Intervening in junior classrooms'. In J.W. Docking (ed) *Alienation in the Junior School*. Basingstoke: Falmer Press.

Cowie, H. and Sharp, S. (1994a) 'Tackling bullying through the curriculum'. In P.K. Smith and S. Sharp (eds) *School Bullying: Insights and Perspectives*. London: Routledge.

Cowie, H. and Sharp, S. (1994b) 'How to tackle bullying through the curriculum'. In S. Sharp and P.K. Smith (eds) *Tackling Bullying in Your School*. London: Routledge.

Cowie, H., Smith, P.K., Boulton, M. and Laver, R. (1994) *Cooperation in the Multi-ethnic Classroom: The Impact of Cooperative Group Work on Social Relationships in Middle Schools*. London: David Fulton.

Croll, P. and Moses, D. (1985) *One in Five*. London: Routledge & Kegan Paul.

Cullingford, C. (1988) 'School rules and children's attitude to discipline'. *Educational Research*, 30, 3–8.

Cullingford, C. (1995) 'Victims of terror'. *Times Educational Supplement*, 13 January.

Department of Education and Science (1989) *Discipline in Schools*. Elton Report. London: HMSO.

Department for Education (1994a) *Pupil Behaviour and Discipline*, Circular 8/94. London: HMSO.

Department for Education (1994b) *The Education of Children with Emotional and Behavioural Difficulties*, Circular 9/94. London: HMSO.

Department for Education (1994c) *Bullying: Don't Suffer in Silence*. London: HMSO.

Department for Education (1994d) *Code of Practice on the Identification and Assessment of Children with Special Educational Needs*. London: HMSO.

Docking, J. W. (1987) *Control and Discipline in Schools: Perspectives and Approaches*, 2nd edn. London: Paul Chapman Publishing.

Docking, J. W. (1990) *Primary Schools and Parents: Rights, Responsibilities and Relationships*. London: Hodder & Stoughton.

Doyle, W. and Carter, K. (1986) 'Academic tasks in classrooms'. In M. Hammersley (ed.) *Case Studies in Classroom Research*. Milton Keynes: Open University Press.

Duax, T. (1988) 'Fostering self-discipline in schools'. *Primary Teaching Studies*, 4, 66–73.

Elliott, M. (1991) 'Bullies,victims, signs, solutions'. In M. Elliott (ed) *Bullying: A Practical Guide to Coping for Schools*. London: Longman.

Fell, G. (1994) 'You're only a dinner lady'. In P. Blatchford and S. Sharp (eds) *Breaktime and the School: Understanding and Changing Playground Behaviour*. London: Routledge.

Ferguson, E. and Houghton, S. (1992) 'The effects of contingent teacher praise, as specified by Canter's Assertive Discipline Programme'. *Educational Studies*, 18, 83–93.

Fincham, F.D. (1983) 'Developmental dimensions in attribution theory'. In J. Jaspers, F.D. Fincham and M. Hewstone (eds) *Attribution Theory and Research*. London: Academic Press.

Fisher, R. (1993) 'Cooperative learning'. *Curriculum*, 14, 23–34.

Fry, P.S. (1987) 'Classroom environments and their effect on problem and non-problem children's classroom behaviour and motivation'. In N. Hastings and J. Schwieso (eds) *New Directions in Educational Psychology: 2. Behaviour and Motivation in the Classroom*. Lewes: Falmer Press.

Galton, M., Simon, B. and Croll, P. (1980) *Inside the Primary school Classroom*. London: Routledge and Kegan Paul

Gasgoigne, E. (1994) 'Special needs can be emotional ones'. Letter to *Times Educational Supplement*, 2 December.

Goldstein, S. and Goldstein, M. (1992) *Hyperactivity*. New York: Wiley.

Gray, J. and Simes, N. (1989) 'Findings from the National Survey of Teachers in England and Wales'. In Department of Education and Science *Discipline in Schools* (The Elton Report). London: HMSO.

Gurney, P. (1990). 'The enhancement of self-esteem in junior classrooms'. In J.W. Docking (ed) *Alienation in the Junior School*. Basingstoke: Falmer Press.

Hargreaves, D.H. (1978) 'What teaching does to teachers'. *New Society*, 9 March, 540–42.

Harrop, A. and Holmes, M. (1993) 'Teachers' perceptions of their pupils' views on rewards and punishments'. *Pastoral Care in Education*, 11, 30–35

Hastings, N. and Schwieso, J. (1994) 'Kindly take your seats', *Times Educational Supplement*, October 21, 3.

H.M. Inspectorate for Schools (1987) *Good Behaviour and Discipline in Schools* (Education Observed 5). London: Department of Education and Science.

Higgins, C. (1994a) 'Improving the school ground environment as an anti-bullying intervention'. In P.K. Smith and S. Sharp (eds) *School Bullying: Insights and Perspectives*. London: Routledge.

Higgins, C. (1994b) 'How to improve the school ground environment as an anti-bullying strategy'. In S. Sharp and P.K. Smith (eds) *Tackling Bullying in Your School*. London: Routledge.

Hinshaw, S.P. (1994) *Attention Deficits and Hyperactivity in Children*. California: Sage.

Hoffman, M.L. (1970) 'Conscience, personality, and socialisation techniques', *Human Development*, 13, 90–126.

Imich, A. and Jefferies, K. (1989) 'The management of lunchtime behaviour'. *Support for Learning*, 4, 46–52.

Jenkin, F. (1989) *Making Small Groups Work*. Oxford: Penguin Educational.

Jones, K. and Lock, M. (1993) 'Working with parents'. In T. Charlton. and K. David (eds)(1993) *Managing Misbehaviour in Schools*, 2nd edn. London: Routledge.

Kagan, S. (1989) *Cooperative Learning: Resources for Teachers*. San Juan Capistrano: Resources for Teachers.

Kagan, J., Mussen, P.H. and Conger, J.J. (1969) *Child Development and Personality*. London: Harper & Row.

Kanouse, D.E., Gumpert, P. and Canavan-Gumpert, D. (1981) 'The semantics of praise'. In J.H. Harvey, W. Ickes and R.F. Kidds (eds) *New Directions in Attribution Research*, vol. 3. Hillsdale: Erlbaum.

Kidscape (n.d.) *Stop Bullying!* London: Kidscape.

Kohlberg, L. (1968) 'The child as moral philosopher'. *Psychology Today*, 2, 25–30.

Kounin, J. (1970) *Discipline and Group Management in Classrooms*. New York: Holt, Rinehart & Winston.

La Fontaine, J. (1991) *Bullying: The Child's View*. London: Calouste Gulbenkian Foundation.

Light, P. (1979) *The Development of Social Sensitivity*. Cambridge: Cambridge University Press.

Little, A.W. (1985) 'The child's understanding of the causes of academic success and failure: a case study of British schoolchildren'. *British Journal of Educational Psychology*, 55, 11–23.

Leech N. and Wooster, A.D. (1986) *Personal and Social Skills*. Exeter: Religious and Moral Education Press.

Lucas, B. (1994) 'The power of school grounds: the philosophy and practice of Learning through Landscapes'. In P. Blatchford and S. Sharp (eds) *Breaktime and the School: Understanding and Changing Playground Behaviour*. London: Routledge.

McGee, R., Sylva, P.A. and Williams, S. (1984) 'Behaviour problems in a population of seven-year-old children'. *British Journal of Educational Psychology*, 55, 11–23.

Maines, B. and Robinson, G. (1992) *The No Blame Approach*. Bristol: Lame Duck.

Merrett, F. and Tang, W.M. (1994) 'The attitudes of British primary school pupils to praise, rewards, punishments and reprimands'. *British Journal of Educational Psychology*, 64, 91–103.

Merrett, F. and Wheldall, K. (1986) 'Natural rates of teacher approval and disapproval in British primary and middle school classrooms'. *British Journal of Educational Psychology*, 57, 95–103.

Mitman, A.L. and Lash, A.A. (1988) 'Students' perceptions of their academic standing and classroom behaviour'. *Elementary School Journal*, 89, 55–68.

Mooney, A., Creeser, R. and Blatchford, P. (1991) 'Children's views on teasing and fighting in junior schools'. *Educational Research*, 33(21), 103–12.

Moriarty, B., Douglas, G., Punch, K. and Hattie, J. (1995) 'The importance of self-efficacy as a mediating variable between learning environments and achievement'. *British Journal of Educational Psychology*, 65, 73–84.

Mortimore, P., Sammons, P., Stoll, L., Lewis, D. and Ecob, R. (1988) *School Matters: The Junior Years*. Wells: Open Books.

Mosley, J. (1992) 'Value added pacts'. *Special Children*, 55, 8–11.

Mosley, J. (1994) *Turn Your School Around*. Wisbech: Learning Development Aids.

Mould, S. (1993) 'Chaos in the classroom'. *Special Children*, 66, 8–11.

National Oracy Project (1990) *Teaching, Talking and Learning in Key Stage One*. York: National Curriculum Council.

Neill, S. R. St. J. (1989) 'The effects of facial expression and posture on children's reported responses to teachers' nonverbal communication'. *British Educational Research Journal*, 15, 195–204.

Neill, S. and Caswell, C. (1993) *Body Language for Competent Teachers*. London: Routledge.

Nicholls, J.G. (1983) 'Conceptions of ability and achievement motivation: a theory and its implications for education'. In G.G. Paris, G.M. Olson and H.W. Stevenson (eds) *Learning and Motivation in the Classroom*. Hillsdale: Erlbaum.

O'Leary, K.D. and O'Leary, S.E. (1977) *Classroom Management*. New York: Pergamon.

Olweus, D. (1993) *Bullying in Schools*. Oxford: Blackwell.

OPTIS (1986) *Lunchtime Supervision*. Oxford: Optis House.

Pellegrini, A.D. and Davis, P.D. (1993) 'Relations between children's playground and classroom behaviour'. *British Journal of Educational Psychology*, 63, 88–95.

Piaget, J. (1932) *The Moral Judgement of the Child*. London: Routledge and Kegan Paul.

Pikas, A. (1989) 'The common concern method of the treatment of mobbing'. In E. Roland and E., Munthe (eds) *Bullying: An International Perspective*. London: David Fulton.

Purkey, W.W. (1970) *Self-concept and School Achievement*. New York: Prentice Hall.

Rogers, C. (1987) 'Attribution theory and motivation in school'. In N. Hastings and J. Schwieso (eds) *New Directions in Educational Psychology: 2 – Behaviour and Motivation in the Classroom*. Lewes: Falmer Press.

Rogers, C. (1990) 'Disaffection in the junior years: a perspective from theories of motivation'. In J.W. Docking (ed) *Alienation in the Junior School*. Basingstoke: Falmer Press.

Rogers, W.A. (1994) *The Language of Discipline*. Plymouth: Northcote House.

Rohrkemper, M. and Brophy, J.E. (1983) 'Teachers' thinking about problem students'. In J. M. Levine and M. C. Wang (eds) *Teacher and Student Perceptions: Implications for Learning*. Hillsdale: Erlbaum.

Rose, J. (1995) 'Subject to scrutiny'. *Times Educational Supplement*, 10 March.

Rosenfield, P., Lambert, N.M. and Black, A. (1985) 'Desk arrangement effects on pupil classroom behaviour'. *Journal of Educational Psychology*, 77, 101–108.

Rosenthal, R. and Jacobson, L. (1968) *Pygmalion in the Classroom*. New York: Holt, Rinehart and Winston.

Ross, C. and Ryan, A. (1990) *Can I Stay In Today, Miss?* Stoke on Trent: Trentham Books.

Ross, C. and Ryan, A. (1994) 'Changing playground society: a whole-school approach'. In P. Blatchford and S. Sharp (eds) *Breaktime and the School: Understanding and Changing Playground Behaviour*. London: Routledge.

Roth, E. E. (1995) 'A clinical and cognitive approach to attention deficits'. *Therapeutic Care and Education*, 3, 41–59.

Schunk, D.H. (1987) 'Self-efficacy and motivated learning? In N. Hastings and J. Schwieso (eds) *New Directions in Educational Psychology: 2. Behaviour and Motivation in the Classroom*. Lewes: Falmer Press.

Sharp, S. (1994) 'Training schemes for lunchtime supervisors in the United Kingdom'. In P. Blatchford and S. Sharp (eds) *Breaktime and the School: Understanding and Changing Playground Behaviour*. London: Routledge.

Sharp, S., Arora, T., Smith, P.K. and Whitney, I. (1994) 'How to measure bullying in your school'. In S. Sharp and P.K. Smith (eds) *Tackling Bullying in Your School*. London: Routledge.

Sharp, S., Cooper, F. and Cowie, H. (1994) 'Making peace in the playground'. In P. Blatchford and S. Sharp (eds) *Breaktime and the School: Understanding and Changing Playground Behaviour*. London: Routledge.

Sharp, S., Cowie, H. and Smith, P.K. (1994) 'How to respond to bullying behaviour'. In S. Sharp and P.K. Smith (eds) *Tackling Bullying in Your School*: London: Routledge.

Sharp, S. and Smith, P.K. (1994) (eds) Tackling Bullying in Your School: London: Routledge

Sharp, S. and Thompson, D. (1994) 'How to establish a whole-school anti-bullying policy'. In S. Sharp and P. K. Smith (eds) *Tackling Bullying in Your School*. London: Routledge.

Sheat, L.G. and Beer, A.R. (1994) 'Giving pupils an effective voice in the design and use of their school grounds'. In P. Blatchford and S. Sharp (eds) *Breaktime and the School: Understanding and Changing Playground Behaviour*. London: Routledge.

Sheridan, M.K. (1991) 'Increasing self-esteem and competency in children'. *International Journal of Early Childhood*, 23, 28–35.

Siann, G., Callaghan, M., Glissov, P., Lockhart, R. and Rawson, I. (1994) 'Who gets bullied? The effect of school, gender and ethnic group'. *Educational Research*, 36, 123–34.

Slavin, R.E. (1990) *Cooperative Learning: Theory, Research and Practice*. Boston: Allyn and Bacon.

Slavin, R. E. (1992) 'Cooperative learning'. In C. Rogers and P. Kutnick (eds) *The Social Psychology of the Primary School*. London: Routledge.

Slee, P.T. (1993) 'Bullying: a preliminary investigation of its nature and the effects of social cognition'. Early Child Development and Care, 87, 47-57

Smith, G. (1994) *The Safer Schools – Safer Cities Bullying Project*. Paper presented to the annual conference of British Psychological Society.

Smith, P.K. and Sharp, S. (1994) 'The problem of school bullying'. In P.K. Smith and S. Sharp (eds) School Bullying: Insights and Perspectives. London: Routledge.

Smith, P.K. and Sharp, S. (eds) (1994) *School Bullying: Insights and Perspectives*. London: Routledge.

Smith, P. K. and Thompson, D. (1991) *Practical Approaches to Bullying*. London: David Fulton.

Stonecroft, M. (1990) *The Speaker's Commission on Citizenship*. London: HMSO.

Tattum, D. and Herbert, G. (1990) *Bullying: A Positive Response*. Cardiff: South Glamorgan Institute.

Thompson, D. and Sharp, S. (1994) *Improving Schools: Establishing and Integrating Whole School Behaviour Policies*. London: David Fulton.

Titman, D. (1993) *Special Places for Special People*. Godalming: Worldwide Fund for Nature/Learning Through Landscapes.

Tizard, B., Blatchford, P., Burke, J., Farquhar, C. and Plewis, L. (1988) *Young Children at School in the Inner City*. Hove: Erlbaum.

Weiner, B. (1979) 'A theory of motivation for some classroom experiences'. *Journal of Educational Psychology*, 71, 3–25.

West, C.M. (1990) 'Waiting for the teacher: the relative effectiveness of procedures used by infant school teachers when children require attention during individual seatwork', *CORE*, 14(1), 4 of 10 microfiche 5E02-8C01.

West, C. and Wheldall, K. (1989) 'Waiting for teacher: the frequency and duration of times children spend waiting for teacher attention in infant school classrooms'. *British Education Research Journal*, 15, 205–16.

Wheldall, K., Bevan, K. and Shortall, K. (1986) 'A touch of reinforcement: the effects of contingent touch on the classroom behaviour of young children', *Educational Review*, 38, 207–16.

Wheldall, K. and Glynn, T. (1989) *Effective Classroom Teaching*. Oxford: Blackwell.

White, M. (1990) 'Circletime', *Cambridge Journal of Education*, 20, 53–56.

White, P. (1988) 'The playground project: a democratic learning experience'. In H. Lauder and P. Brown (eds) *Education in Search of a Future*. Basingstoke: Falmer Press.

Whitney, I. and Smith, P.K. (1993) 'A survey of the nature and extent of bully/victim problems in junior/middle and secondary schools', *Educational Research*, 35, 3–25.

Whitney, I., Rivers, I., Smith, P.K. and Sharp,S. (1994) 'The Sheffield Project: methodology and findings'. In P.K. Smith and S. Sharp (eds) *School Bullying: Insights and Perspectives*. London: Routledge.

Wragg, T.(1993) *Primary Teaching Skills*. London: Routledge.

Index